The New Normal

THE New Normal

Living as a
Frum Jew in a
Crazy World

REBBETZIN FEIGE TWERSKI

MOSAICA PRESS

Mosaica Press, Inc.

© 2016 by Mosaica Press

Designed and typeset by Rayzel Broyde

ISBN-10: 1-937887-74-X

ISBN-13: 978-1-937887-74-2

Published and distributed by:

Mosaica Press, Inc.

www.mosaicapress.com

info@mosaicapress.com

This book is dedicated to my children who, despite the mistakes I made along the way, turned out to be the most remarkable and wonderful human beings in the world.

May the רבונו של עולם grant that their children will give them no less nachas than they have given us.

Table of Contents

APPROBATION

A Husband's Thoughts about His Rebbetzin's Book

RAV MICHEL TWERSKI, SHLITA

N o one need feel sorry for me.

I come from a family of high achievers, siblings whose brilliance and accomplishments are of international renown. From my earliest years, people would inquire, "Are you Reb Shloime's or Reb Motel's brother?" Knowing how well-thought of they were, I was proud to answer in the affirmative. **Pride by association — one.**

Some years later that transitioned into, "Are you Dr. Abraham Joshua Twerski's brother?" Once again, knowing his fame as a psychiatrist and prolific author, I answered "Yes" with a firm voice. **Pride by association — two.**

Then my twin brother, Professor Aaron Twerski, made it big as Dean of Hofstra Law School and as a leading legal authority in product liability law, just to name a couple of the things on his extensive list of scholarly achievements. Again (in this case because there was an additional complication of resemblance), I was asked, "Are you Professor

Twerski's brother?" And once again I responded proudly, "Yes, I am."
Pride by association — three.

To my great credit, I had learned to accept my "distinction by association" with admirable poise and aplomb, refusing to interpret my anonymity as a commentary on my personal worth. So, in the best tradition of "smile, things could be worse," I smiled, and sure enough … things got worse.

My very inspired and talented Rebbetzin began writing articles that resonated with women across the world and thus attained global recognition. She was invited to speak all over America and Europe, and her articles morphed into two popular books published by ArtScroll's Mesorah division. Predictably, I was now being introduced as … Rebbetzin Feige's husband. **Pride by association — four.**

But, remember, I began my introduction by asserting that no one need feel sorry for me.

The reason for that is that the Twerski family mantra, from the cradle onward, was, "Work hard at being the very best 'you' who you can be, because that's all that matters. Hashem does not mark on the curve." We were raised on the story of our illustrious forbearer, Reb Zisha of Anapolie, *zt"l*, who told his chassidim that he was not afraid if, after his earthly sojourn, Hashem would ask him, "Zisha, why weren't you as great as Moshe Rabbeinu, or Rabbi Akiva, or the Baal Shem Tov?" He felt confident that he could defend himself adequately against those questions. Reb Zisha said that what he feared most was Hashem saying to him, "Zisha, why weren't you Zisha?"

I am proud of and happy for my brothers that they are who they are, but at the same time, I am also in the process of working at becoming the very best me I can become, and that is such a full-time job that I have no time for invidious comparisons. My fervent hope and prayer is that when my journey is over, I will have the pride of being identified as the "me" Hashem wanted me to be. **Pride by realization.**

At the core of my Rebbetzin's work is the conviction that every individual, regardless of gender, has an inner integrity that is holy, pure, capable, and effective, and that is accessible in every avenue of life to enable us to enjoy life to the fullest. Her conclusion in this regard is that this end can only be attained by our determination to be ourselves.

I encourage everyone who peruses this very wise, down-to-earth, practical, and insightful collection of articles to deeply breathe in that which it has to offer. It will, beyond a doubt, enrich your life and the lives of your loved ones in ways that will enable you to cope effectively with the contemporary challenges of *The New Normal*.

Introduction

A wise man once said, "Friendship is born at that moment when one person says to another: 'What, you too? I thought I was the only one.'"

My work is premised on the feeling that we are all "friends;" and that human experience, however variegated and nuanced, is more or less the same for all of us. Despite our many superficial differences, we are of a single fabric, trying to cope with life's challenges and struggles as we strive toward a common destiny. It is my hope that the insights recorded in this manuscript that have resonated with me will be helpful and resonate with you, my dear readers, as well.

This basic supposition is reflected every week in our shul, after my husband, *shlita*, finishes sharing a *devar Torah* with the *mispallelim*, when, without fail, they line up to "accuse" him of directing his remarks personally at them. Invariably they say something along the lines of, "Rabbi, I know you were talking to me," to which my husband replies, "I was actually talking to myself and letting everyone eavesdrop."

It is in this spirit that this book is offered.

As many of my readers know, the thoughts collected in this volume appeared originally in my weekly column of *Ami* magazine. I am grateful to the *Ami* staff for collecting my articles from their archives so that they might appear in this publication.

There are some special people who contributed very substantially to the publication of this book, and I am indebted to them beyond words.

Rabbi Yaacov Haber, *shlita*, the driving force behind Mosaica Press, motivated me to submit my recent work for publication, not allowing me to rest on the laurels of my first two books, published by ArtScroll. My husband and I first met Rabbi Haber many years ago when we taught at a Shabbaton in Buffalo, New York, where Rabbi Haber was a shul rav and chief *mekarev*. We have watched with great *nachas* Rabbi Haber's emergence as a scholar and visionary, whose work is appreciated everywhere in the Jewish world. We treasure the friendship of the Rabbi and his wonderful Rebbetzin Bayle, and pray for their continued success in their every endeavor.

In addition, Rabbi Doron Kornbluth, senior editor of Mosaica Press, was a tireless organizer, supervisor, and communicator. He ensured that I didn't drop the ball and he oversaw the exquisite details of finding the common denominators in the articles to help them come together in a synergistic and eminently accessible way.

Going back a bit further, I owe a debt of gratitude to Reb Nechemia Coopersmith of aish.com, who, despite my resistance, launched my writing career by "nudging" me persistently to put my thoughts to paper. A better "nudge" there never was. Rechy Frankfurter, first as founder of *Binah* magazine and most recently as editor of *Ami* magazine, provided constant encouragement and a venue for sharing the ideas and counsel found in this book. She has been a marvelous friend and remarkable cheerleader. Yoni Schlussel, a beloved member of our community, has always been available with the utmost graciousness and patience to type my articles. Yoni's expeditious and glad-hearted response to converting my dictation to print has made a weekly challenge not only doable, but pleasurable as well. Finally, a special *yasher koach* to my husband, who, despite his heavy schedule, has been a true partner in reviewing and editing my work.

Most importantly, I am grateful to the *Ribbono Shel Olam* for the wherewithal to share insights that I hope will be helpful to my fellow travelers on our journey towards a better us and a better world. If anything I have written or said has enriched even one life, I will consider that a *zechus* far more precious than any of the world's greatest material treasures.

CHAPTER 1

Energy In

I n a quiet suburb on the outskirts of Milwaukee, there is a small, family-owned business where I frequently shop. Though neither the proprietors nor the personnel are Jewish, they have always treated me and other frum Jewish customers with the greatest deference and courtesy. From time to time they express curiosity about our religious practices, which they unfailingly receive with genuine interest and admiration.

As I was checking out during a recent visit, Michael, one of the proprietor's sons, initiated a conversation. Since he had always impressed me as a fine and sensitive young man, I listened respectfully. He shared with me his frustration about his parents who, he claimed, refused to "get with the times." He complained that they insisted on holding onto outmoded beliefs and conventions that were honored in the past, steadfastly refusing to acknowledge that the world has moved on and that out of necessity, they must adjust their thinking to accommodate the changes.

While it is impossible to argue with the massive impact of technology on our culture, I attempted to frame and justify his parents' perspective in the context of values. Certainly, cell phones, the "web,"

Skype, and modern advances of all types have taken over the world, and in many ways have benefited contemporary communication.

The caveat, however, I told him, is that we dare not extrapolate from the technological world to our spiritual existence. The advances and progress in the physical realm are ones we can consider embracing, with certain limitations. After all, none of us want to go back to the pony express or wood-burning stoves! The danger, however, is thinking that the same surrender to technology applies to our time-honored moral principles and sacred values.

Sadly, our society has adopted an attitude of "morality by consensus," that of people voting (literally and figuratively) on moral issues, and believing that their vote should determine whether the codes and standards that have elevated human conduct throughout history are still relevant.

In recent times, for the most part, Western civilization has demonstrated little respect for the fact that moral criteria come from a Higher Authority, a Wisdom far greater than our own, and that we don't have the prerogative to vote on them or alter them according to our changing times.

I suggested to Michael that our current attitude towards morality is so preposterous that it is tantamount to someone insisting that the law of gravity was outmoded, and that he is indeed capable of jumping off a rooftop, convinced he will soar upward instead of falling downward. We all know how unfortunate that would be! Defying physical laws that govern the existence of the world is not only ill-advised but is ultimately catastrophic.

Can you vote against the law of gravity?

Similarly, the 613 mitzvos for Jews — and the seven Noachide laws for non-Jews — ordered by the Master of the World, serve as the foundation and underpinning of the universe. To ignore, disregard, or violate these fundamental, G-d-given principles is no less devastating and tragic than trying to defy principles of physics.

The legalization of "alternative" lifestyles, abortion rights, and the growing support for euthanasia are symptomatic of the deterioration of the moral fiber of our society.

The liberal attitude represented by Michael's contention that it is everyone's right to choose whatever makes him happy (regardless of the cost) has great appeal. The very idea that there are values that supersede one's pleasure is anathema to the Michaels of our culture: It is all about "me."

Given the constant assault on Jewish values, we must be ever more vigilant not to let our sensitivities become dulled such that we respond with a lesser feeling of outrage to the ethical travesties of our time.

It is crucial that we maintain clarity as to what is right and what is wrong.

Still, what makes arguing the traditional perspective so complicated and frustrating is that the "Michaels" that surround us are not demons with horns. Many of them are good and decent — albeit misguided — human beings. This makes it all the more challenging to eschew their views and maintain one's uncompromised commitment to what we know to be true and non-negotiable.

Interestingly, while Michael thought his views were new and his parents' were old, history tells a different story.

I recall an encounter that took place between my father, the Faltishener Rav, *zt"l*, and David Ben Gurion, who was, at the time, Israel's Prime Minister.

The two found themselves on the same flight to Israel. During the course of the flight, as my father was putting on *tallis* and *tefillin*, Ben Gurion walked by and muttered under his breath, "These antiquated Jews who insist on hanging on to archaic practices of the past."

My father, not one to ever suffer insults quietly (especially if leveled against his treasured tradition), responded instantly by saying,

Quite the contrary, Mr. Prime Minister. Between the two of us, you are far more old-fashioned than I am. You may pride yourself on being modern and progressive, but let me remind you that Terach, the idolatrous predecessor of the Patriarch Avraham, came long before the Torah and mitzvos to which I ascribe. In the Passover Hagaddah we annually read, "In the beginning our ancestors were idolators, Terach, the father of Avraham."

You, Mr. Prime Minister, are a throwback to those pre-Sinai primitive times, while my practices are far more recent.

Mr. Prime Minister, you are far more old-fashioned than I am.

Simply put, my father's reply encapsulated the thought that answering to nothing other than one's own base desires ("anything goes") is really just an expression of one of the oldest human failings — the rejection of authority. This is not a new idea indeed, it is a relic of an uncivilized, ancient time; in a sense, it is the very philosophy that Judaism exists to defeat.

The great longevity and technological presence of this "you do what you want and I do what I want" mentality demonstrates its great power. All of this demands that we be aware of rationalizations and the powerful force of self-interest that blinds us to the point where the abhorrent becomes acceptable. The Prophet Yeshayahu perhaps says it best, "Woe to those who call evil good and who call good evil; who make darkness into light, and light into darkness, who say that bitter is sweet, and sweet is bitter" (*Yeshayahu* 5:20).

A couple of years ago, my hometown of Milwaukee, along with much of the Midwest and other parts of the country, was subjected to extraordinary rainstorms and hail. We were bombarded with constant warnings to prepare for flash flooding, despite the fact that no one knew exactly how to prepare for an event of such magnitude. As was predicted, the rains came. Our basement flooded, and we had to have water removed from the carpeting on more than one occasion. This was all the more disconcerting because my husband's study and Torah library are located in the basement. Fortunately, however, the bookshelves had been built high enough off the floor that despite the huge quantities of water that managed to seep inside, his *sefarim* weren't damaged.

Many scientists described this latest weather phenomenon as the "new normal," and all of its ramifications, they assert, are a result of our having dealt with our environment in too cavalier a manner. Now, they wag their fingers, we are paying the price for not adequately respecting our surroundings.

It struck me that the "new normal" applies not only to weather but to the general landscape of our lives. The entire moral and ethical structure of contemporary society is barely recognizable when compared to that of only a few decades ago. In contrast to its physical counterpart (the floods, for example), this "new normal" in our culture goes virtually uncontested. Alternative lifestyles and the way people talk, dress, and comport themselves are but some of its conspicuously disturbing features. Tragically, most people have settled into a mindset of unquestioning acceptance.

The "new normal" in our culture of "anything goes" is virtually uncontested.

I often think of the reaction people of the last generation would have if they were to come back and experience our "brave new world." Aside from the more noxious violations of conscience, even the innocuous scene of people hardly communicating with each other because of their preoccupation with technological devices would horrify them.

The Talmud relates the story of the great sage, Choni Hama'agal, who was subjected by a Heavenly decree to sleep for seventy years. Upon awakening, he found himself in a world he could not recognize and one with which he had little in common. He entered the *beis hamedrash*, the communal house of learning, figuring that perhaps there he would find the comfort of a familiar setting. To his dismay, his scholarly opinion was ignored, even when the Talmudic authority quoted was himself! Ultimately, feeling totally out of place and irrelevant, he prayed for Hashem to take him from this world.

In a similar vein, I recently received a letter from an older woman who was trying to come to terms with what she observed as a drastic departure from the proprieties with which she had grown up. Specifically, she lamented the change of attitude of children toward their elders. She wasn't referring to "problem" children; she contended that even mainstream children from "fine" homes interacted in an all-too-familiar manner with their parents. In her opinion, it was a manifestation of a cultural shift in the area of *kibbud av va'eim*, with a discernible diminution in formal expressions of respect. She maintained that the sort of behavior going on in her own children's homes would not have been tolerated in her formative years. With great pain and distress, she sought to understand what was happening to the sacred way of life we once enjoyed. Clearly, she was not adjusting to the "new normal."

Troubling as the "new normal" in the weather department may be, it goes without saying that the threat to the values and ideals that have hallowed the Jewish People since our consecration as Hashem's select nation is by far the greater issue. The only consolation for me is our Sages' statement that one of the telltale signs of Moshiach's coming is that the generation will be characterized by chutzpah and an attitude of brazenness. Since the drift of the "new normal" appears to be going in that direction, then the good news is that Moshiach can't be very far behind.

Consider the experience of Abby, who voiced to me her deep concern over the "other party" in her husband's life, a presence that has alienated his affection and attention to the point where their marriage is being threatened. She identified the intruder as "digital insanity" — her husband's obsession with iPhones, iPads, etc. — an all-encomapssing attachment to these devices that keeps him from ever being fully present with her and the family. She claims that the "I" of these phones, pads, and the like has replaced the "we," the togetherness that had always been the bedrock of her family. Unquestionably, the ever-escalating and undisciplined preoccupation with this "digital insanity" has wreaked havoc not only with the general level of happiness of families, but has corrupted the personal integrity of the individual, as well. Abby lamented that in her estimation, it is the scourge — indeed, the idolatry — of our times.

How do we stop the onslaught of world-
views antithetical to Torah?

In a desperate attempt to combat this pernicious influence, *"chareidi"* communities have tried to build walls, self-imposed ghettos of sorts, where the hope is that they will keep the modern world's negative influences at bay.

One must respect these intentions. They certainly emanate from a holy place. Yet, however laudable the effort, one cannot underestimate the power of this digital and cultural tsunami, a veritable tidal wave of pollution that everyone inhales with every breath. In my humble estimation, the dams and levies have so far, in the main, been unsuccessful in stemming the flood waters of morally corrosive viewpoints and attitudes.

Perhaps a more advisable approach for our times, where insulation and isolation are virtually impossible in almost all cases, is to fortify ourselves and our families by way of greater immersion in Torah learning. More than ever, one needs to find mentors who are knowledgable, wise, and broad-minded; Torah personalities with whom a person can be open and free to discuss his conflicts and to share whatever is on his mind.

Mentors must avoid being judgmental. They should appreciate

the challenges of a time in history about which the Satmar Rebbe, Reb Yoel, *zt"l*, said is one in which walking down a single block is fraught with more *"nisyonos"* than a lifetime in Europe of old. It is hard — but together, with Hashem's help, and by clinging to Torah authorities, we can indeed stay normal, despite the "new normal."

There is another way to limit the contemporary onslaught against Jewish values.

The thought came to me at 9:30 one Shabbos morning, as I subconsciously waited for my friend Sandy to come pick me up on the way to shul, as she has done for the better part of fifty years. Of course, her knock on the door never materialized, as she had recently moved to Israel.

I sat for awhile reflecting on why Sandy is so special to me. *Baruch Hashem*, I am surrounded by a community of people who are wonderful and amazing, each in his or her own right. I have been friends with many of them for decades and enjoy being with them all. Each of them is special. Sandy, for instance, is easy to be with. When she walks into a room the sun starts to shine, even on cloudy days. Sandy has not been jaded by life; she maintains a refreshing aura of innocence and optimism, and not because of a dearth of challenges or a privileged existence. Sandy has paid her dues, but they have not suppressed her love of life and *emunah peshutah*. In fact, her faith never wavers. Sandy is straightforward and I rely on her opinion and uncompromising honesty. Whenever she has told me I made a bad purchase, for example, she has always been right.

Sandy relishes and celebrates the joys and good fortunes of others. My father, *z"l*, often suggested that in response to all the ills of the world a *"farginners'* club" should be formed of people dedicated to being happy for others' good luck. Membership cards could be issued and kept in one's wallet along with his driver's license and credit cards. This, my father insisted, would mitigate many of the tragedies that befall us, *r"l*.

Sandy would unquestionably be a shoo-in for president of such a club.

This mood of reflection produced another image, that of my niece Mimi. Mimi is the daughter of my husband's oldest brother, Reb Shlomo, z"l. She does not live anywhere near me, but we have managed to have a meaningful and intimate long-distance relationship for many years. Reb Shlomo was a towering giant of the spirit. He had a tragic life, one which was marked by great suffering. And yet, his presence was electrifying, speaking of an otherworldly existence. Observers had a sense that he had a connection to the supernal realms that was far beyond the grasp of ordinary human beings.

Mimi is a low-keyed, less intimidating version of her father. While totally grounded, intuitive, and people-oriented, there is a G-d-consciousness about her that permeates her person. Her comfort level with the Master of the Universe is effortless and appears to be second nature. There is a Jewish saying , "For believers there are no questions, and for non-believers there are no answers." Despite her many challenges and struggles over the years, Mimi has never voiced any questions. She exudes an acceptance, peace, and serenity that is calming to all who encounter her. I love being with Mimi. In her presence, I am reminded of the words of a famous poem: "I love you not only for who you are, but for who I am when I am with you." She brings Heaven down to earth. There is neither posturing nor pretense, only genuine goodness and an unmistakable abiding faith. When I am with her, I find myself aspiring to greater things.

Why do I share with you these vignettes about only a few of my friends?

Friends are crucial. In fact, the importance of making friends is underscored many times in our holy *sefarim*. Consider the results of the configuration of the Twelve Tribes' encampment in the desert. The *Midrash Tanchuma*, cited by Rashi on *Bamidbar* 3:28, tells us about the price paid by the tribe of Reuven because they were located near the Levite tribe of Kehos. As a consequence of their proximity, Dasan, Aviram, and 250 others were adversely influenced by Korach. "Woe to the wicked, and woe to his neighbor!" our Sages exclaimed. Conversely, as Rashi continues, the tribes of Yissaschar and Zevulun were positively influenced by being close to Moshe and Aharon and became renowned for their great piety and Torah scholarship. "Fortunate are the righteous, fortunate are their neighbors" is the rule here. This truth is further emphasized by Rabbi Yehoshua in *Pirkei Avos* (2:13) in his answer to the question of his teacher, Rabbi Yochanan ben Zakkai, regarding the best acquisition a person should seek. He answered: "a good friend."

Environment and context are powerful forces in determining who we are and who we will become. "Show me your friends and I will tell you who you are" is an apt observation.

In the morning davening we ask Hashem to distance us from "a bad person, a bad friend, etc." This *tefillah* speaks to an understanding of how crucial it is to surround ourselves with people who bring positive energy into our lives.

As we have seen, and as we can all-too-easily see, the world at large is full of many toxic influences. At the very least, our inner space, our immediate environment, should serve as an oasis of goodness and G-dliness.

> *The world is full of many toxic influences. At the very least, our immediate environment — and in particular, our friends — should serve as an oasis.*

While much of the toxicity surrounding us today is relatively new, by definition humans have always struggled with keeping their heads "in the right places" and not being influenced by negativity and noxious attitudes. Consider the following idea:

Among the many *berachos* a Torah-observant Jew recites in the course of an ordinary day is a most remarkable blessing called *"Asher Yatzar."* The benediction gratefully acknowledges Hashem's providence over our body's ability to cleanse itself of impurities and waste products.

Although we generally accept this process as routine (with the result that the *berachah* sometimes suffers from being taken for granted), it is truly a most critical recognition of Hashem's wondrous intervention in our lives.

My father-in-law, the Hornosteipler Rebbe, *zt"l*, recounted that a patient suffering from kidney failure once told him that he felt this *berachah* should be recited with the same solemnity that is associated with *Kol Nidrei* on Yom Kippur Eve: One should take out a *sefer Torah* and put on a *tallis* and *kittel* to express appreciation for G-d's manifest kindness to our body.

An equally remarkable (but somehow less celebrated) phenomenon is the similar function of the human psyche to discriminate between the useful and the wasteful, the restorative and the toxic, the joyful and the depressing, and thus purge our minds from impurities that do not serve us well.

In the spiritual and emotional realm, no less than in the the physical, G-d has blessed us with the ability to choose good health and well-being, to let go of our contaminated thinking, and choose relief by not holding on to hurts and resentments that cause painful and emotional impaction.

Nancy came into therapy feeling emotionally obstructed and tortured. For years, ever since her marriage at the tender age of seventeen, she had suffered subtle abuse at the hands of her mother-in-law, Gail. Whether it was the way she dressed, how and what she cooked, or the size of her family, Nancy found she could do little that was right in her mother-in-law's eyes. What exacerbated the situation was that Gail was seen as a virtuous individual by the world at large, so that no one could believe that Nancy was the victim of her mother-in-law's disparagement. Nancy, now a middle-aged woman with children and grandchildren of her own, and whose mother-in-law is long gone, sought relief from the "toxic" lingering effects of that unfortunate relationship.

In therapy, Nancy began to understand that as long as she kept reliving the past hurts, aside from the unnecessary pain she was inflicting on herself, she was also giving her deceased mother-in-law continued power over her life. She also gained an appreciation for the fact that, as someone once put it, harboring anger and resentment against someone is like "drinking poison and hoping that the other person dies." Unquestionably, the only victim is the one who harbors those toxic feelings. In addition, Eleanor Roosevelt's apt observation, "Nobody can make us feel inadequate without our permission," became an oft-consulted and healing maxim in her life.

Nancy also came to the realization that her mother-in-law's unfortunate interaction with her was a product of the older woman's own misery, i.e., manifold rejections in her own life. It became clear that her lashing out was not about Nancy, but came from her own unresolved trauma. As this understanding deepened, Nancy began to come closer to a place where she was increasingly able to replace feelings of resentment with feelings of compassion whenever she thought of Gail.

Hearing over and over again the concept that it is our thinking and not our circumstances that creates our reality had a tremendous impact. The idea that we are thinkers — and hence in the driver's seat — was liberating to Nancy. Her state of "emotional occlusion" was slowly relieved, and the toxins in her psyche no longer poisoned her existence. She exuded a new health and vitality. Now, when she recites "*Asher Yatzar*," she thanks Hashem for the miraculous ability to free her body from noxious materials and the equally miraculous capacity to free her consciousness from detrimental memories and thinking.

We can each do the same. We are not victims of the past or the present. We can free ourselves of past and present traumas and attitudes that cloud our daily lives. Through good friends, healthy communities, and a strong commitment to Torah learning and prayer, we can bring emotional and spiritual health to ourselves and to those around us, and thus avoid the negativity of the "brave new world."

Our Sages make a puzzling statement (*Baitza* 16a) about Babylonian culture, one of the progenitors of Western civilization: "How foolish are the Babylonians, who eat bread with bread."

"How foolish are the Babylonians, who eat
bread with bread."

There are many commentaries who expound on this puzzling observation. Clearly, this cannot be an assessment of an undesirable diet, i.e., that the Babylonians are being criticized for overloading on carbs. I happen to know many otherwise smart Jews who enjoy their carbs, and frankly, I myself would likely be a "bread-with-bread" consumer, were it not for the dietary experts who caution against such a diet.

My son, Reb Efraim, suggested the following interpretation: He noted that were the Babylonians to be asked why they eat bread, meaning "food" in general, they would undoubtedly say that they do so in order to have the energy to work.

If then one were to further inquire why they need to work, their response would be so that they would be able to afford to put bread on their table.

Hence, life for them is reduced to this unending cycle of eating to work and working to eat — a steady diet of "bread with bread." "Bread-with-bread" becomes the pathetic mantra, the lamentable sum-total of their lives. Unquestionably, an existence so devoid of substance deserves the Talmudic condemnation of being "foolish" at the very least, and tragic, at most. A prominent thinker put it this way: "To die is poignantly bitter, but the idea of having to die without having lived is unbearable."

"How fortunate are we, and how pleasant is our lot" is David Hamelech's exclamation when observing the life of the Jew. Of course, the Jewish People also eat bread. We, too, work hard to earn an honest living and pray daily that Hashem should bless us with all good things, spiritually *and* materially. However, we understand the incontrovertible fact that one cannot, and indeed, should not, live on bread alone. Our *neshamos* must be given their due, their adequate sustenance, if we are to find our earthly existence tolerable and worthwhile.

This particularly Jewish phenomenon impressed itself upon me once when my husband and I were invited to be "Scholars in Residence" at an idyllic winter resort where there was no dearth of *"olam hazeh"* provisions. The general area was breathtakingly beautiful and offered many appealing tourist sites and attractions. The hotel appointments were lovely, the grounds stunning, and the food capable of driving a Babylonian to such excess that he would explode.

One would have assumed that the guests (all *heimishe/chareidi Yidden*) would have been inclined to take a break from their regular pressured and disciplined routines and indulge themselves uninhibitedly during this short respite. Instead, early in the morning, clusters of *chavrusas* were visible everywhere, learning their daily *shiurim* with fervor and enthusiasm. In the evening, they once again attended *shiurim*, sitting in the *beis hamedrash* until late into the night. To be sure, they were on vacation, but their Torah learning and warm davening surely were not.

The declaration *"Mi k'amcha Yisrael,"* who can compare to Your nation Israel, flashed across this group of vacationers with breathtaking force. There is, indeed, no other nation like Hashem's people. The world we live in is largely focused on bread for the sake of bread.

Jewish survival over generations of being subjected to savage persecution testifies that *Yidden* aren't "bread-with-bread" consumers. The physical bread of *Klal Yisrael* is secondary and incidental to that which truly drives our lives. Watching our Torah-observant men and women at the hotel, I felt privileged and proud to be part of so exalted a nation. I believe that the *Ribbono Shel Olam* cannot help but notice the passionate devotion of His people to His will and instruction. For this inspired nation, we offer our *tefillah* that at long last Hashem will gather us to His home where, undistracted by those whose existence is all about eating "bread-with-bread," we will be free to focus on the purpose of bread — our *avodas Hashem*.

A nation like this, only a nation like this, can stay pure and focused on its mission, regardless of the increasing levels of toxicity that surround us.

CHAPTER 2

Energy Out

There are certain moments in our lives that are impactful and transformative. Those of us who are old enough probably remember exactly where we were and what we were doing when President Kennedy was assassinated, or more recently, when we learned of the tragedy of 9/11.

One of those moments etched in my memory was a visit from London by my husband's first cousin, which occurred early in my married life. Chayke was tall and lovely; she was a very formal and proper Englishwoman. I was standing in my kitchen preparing dinner when she suddenly walked in and dissolved into tears.

I was taken aback.

Aside from the fact that I barely knew her, her behavior was in stark contrast to her usually reserved, private, and regal manner. She had just lost her husband. Mendele had not been ill, and his passing was sudden. She broken-heartedly shared that it was not so much his death, difficult as it was to accept, that haunted her, but the fact that (because she had expected him to always be there) she hadn't taken the time to tell him how much he meant to her. Mendele had been a quiet, unassuming man, the solid rock of her existence. She had somehow come to take him for granted. It was the words left unspoken that rendered her inconsolable.

Almost fifty years have passed since that encounter, but her words left an indelible impression on me. It is a human tendency to postpone acknowledging the people closest to us; we somehow assume that they must already know how much they mean to us.

Additionally, the demands and frenetic pace of life usually have us attending to immediate "pressing" issues, leaving that which should be top priority for another time. Someone aptly cautioned that the more important things in life should not be at the mercy of the lesser ones.

Naomi Remen, a noted secular psychiatrist now in her eighties, noted that it was her *zeide* who had the greatest impact on her life. It was he who loved her unconditionally and blessed her every Friday night, calling her "*neshamaleh*," his beloved little soul. He passed away when she was only seven, but his memory informed her entire life. In contrast to her grandfather's love and support, she and her achievements were never enough for her parents, who were the consummate professionals. If she scored ninety-seven on a test, they wanted to know what happened to the other three points.

She reflected sadly that she had spent her entire life trying to make them happy. On her mother's deathbed, Naomi finally confided her great pain. She told her mother that ever since her grandfather had died, she had felt that nobody valued her or blessed her.

Her mother's response is probably one of the saddest statements imaginable. She said, "I have blessed you every day of your life. I just didn't have the good sense to say it out loud so you could hear it."

Erich Fromm, the famous sociologist and psychoanalyst, points out that in His creation of the world, G-d provided a paradigm for us to follow. Not only did He bring the universe into being by the pronouncement of "Let there be light, a firmament, vegetation ..." but He followed up with an affirmation: "and G-d saw that it was good."

Similarly, Fromm posits, in the creation of our personal worlds, we should not only attend to the basic needs of those around us but should follow them up with assurances that *they are good*. Especially mothers and caregivers, he states, who most closely resemble the function of the earth, can either simply provide the basic milk of sustenance or, hopefully, emulate the "land flowing with milk and honey."

> *Do we provide others only with the "milk" of*
> *their basic needs or also the "honey" of sweet*
> *affirmation?*

"Honey" refers to positive words and comments of affirmation, how blessed and fortunate we are to have these people in our lives — a variance of "it was good." His concluding observation is that an individual's sense of self testifies as to whether he was raised solely on the "milk" of basic nurturance, or if the sweetness of "honey" was also part of his experience.

The point is that, as busy and hassled as we are, we need to make time to notice those around us, especially those entrusted to our sphere of care and influence. Furthermore, noticing them is not enough — we need to proactively compliment them and share our positive feelings about them.

We all need affirmation. Words of affirmation escort us throughout our lives. They warm us during the cold winter nights of our existence. And it doesn't require a great expenditure of time and energy; all it takes is mindfulness.

One of the things I admire most about my daughter Baila is that she immediately acknowledges anything that is done for her with a card, note, or phone call. Admittedly, although I have good intentions and totally appreciate the many kindnesses extended to me, I am still working on following my daughter's example. I want to — and will (G-d willing!) — do this more.

How often should we "be positive?" Psychologists have suggested that in our interactions with our loved ones, every critical comment should be balanced by at least five positive ones.

> *Every critical comment should be balanced
> by at least five positive ones.*

Doing so benefits those we compliment and accomplishes even more: in extending both "milk and honey," we become better people. We bring excellence to our own humanity.

I think all of us have experienced an intuitive, visceral reaction at the mention of certain people's names or actually seeing any of these same individuals in person.

On the up-side, some people are the bearers of a bright and positive energy. I have friends who make me smile even before they say anything amusing, and others have such generous, giving natures that I am warmed just by being in their presence. Some people are blessed with a rare emotional intelligence that is transmitted in finely nuanced ways. Others inspire confidence in us, and we automatically feel free to confide in them and solicit their advice.

Many people have shared with me how my sister Chaya (the Tzeilemer Rebbetzin), conjures up the image of a "queen mother" ministering to her kingdom, while my sister Blima (true to her name, which means "flower") immediately fills a room with her engaging personality. The fragrance of her person exudes vitality and an embrace of life that is uplifting.

Then, of course, there are inevitably some people to whom we react differently, those who have either deliberately or inadvertently brought sullen, negative energy into our lives. The mere thought of them makes us cringe.

For example, when Esther speaks of her mother-in-law, who is long deceased, the simple mention of her name brings a shadow of pain to her face. Although her mother-in-law no doubt had many wonderful qualities, she was mean-spirited and critical when it came to Esther. On a cognitive level, Esther knows that this dark presence in her life is gone. Viscerally, though, the damaging memories continue to have an adverse effect on her.

Abby was one of those people whose victim mentality made her feel shortchanged in life. The result was that she begrudged others the good that was theirs and therefore not hers. She brought an *"ayin ra'ah,"* literally, a "bad eye," a jaundiced view of life, to every encounter. Needless to say, people did not relish or warmly anticipate her presence.

The point of examining how the people in our lives affect us is to check our *middos* — always an important activity for a Jew. Moving forward is achieved by taking a good, hard look at ourselves. I would venture to say that what our presence evokes in others is a reliable barometer of our *"bein adam la'chaveiro,"* our interpersonal relationships and general spiritual well-being. If we find that there is a deficiency in this area, the likelihood is that our relationship with Hashem is suffering as well. The litmus test to which we might subject ourselves is to objectively observe the reaction of the significant people in our lives to our presence. These would include husbands, children, parents, friends, and business associates. Does a positive energy escort us, or do we bring black clouds wherever we go? Do people seem happy to see us? Does our appearance bring a smile to their lips and a sparkle to their eyes?

If not, we have work to do. The good news is that self-awareness gives us the tools to alter the energies we exude and therefore improve the dynamics of our relationships.

I have a personal confession to make. Our Sages counsel us to strive for balance in our interactions with our children, advising *"smol dochah v'yamin mekareves,"* the left hand should push away while the right hand draws close.

Ostensibly, they mean that there is a simultaneous need for both discipline and love. Typically, a mother's role (for better and for worse) is seeing to it that her children "toe the line." Being the primary nurturer who spends the most time with her offspring naturally translates into the necessity to act as the enforcer of the rules of proper behavior. Predictably, this is not conducive to winning a popularity contest. Fathers, who spend the bulk of their time either learning or working, enjoy the privilege of waltzing into the house and embracing their children with unconditional love, free of the judgment and criticism a mother must often voice as part of her parenting role. While it is true that in some instances the roles are reversed, this is the case more often than not.

For the most part, my own situation has reflected the classic role of being the "heavy" in the family. My husband's fortunate stance, borne largely of his preoccupation with learning, in addition to catering to and counseling others, has permitted him to be impervious to the brief and passing negative stages in our children's lives. Of course, this has frequently left me "holding the bag." There is no question that our children's respect and love extend equally to both of us. If there is a difference at all, it is subtle at best. Nonetheless, immediately upon entering the house or calling on the phone they inquire, "Where's Tatty?" or "Where is Zaidy?" Literally and figuratively, they seek the embrace of unconditional love. Of course, they look for Mommy and Bobbi "also," which in my more sensitive and vulnerable moments is cause for chagrin — I am an "also!"

I have often jokingly commented to my children that in the next *gilgul* (reincarnation) I want to be the oblivious, non-confrontational, loving "Tatty." Until then, I have been working on myself to adopt a more even-tempered attitude of total acceptance. If I notice a departure in their behavior that I deem inappropriate, I address it to the Master of the World. I ask Him to intervene on their behalf and give them clarity. Obviously, it is in His power to do that which I cannot. This makes me feel better and lessens the heavy, prosecutorial sense of responsibility. Moreover, I no longer feel upset that my husband can enjoy the "*yamin mekareves*" role in a way that did not formerly seem available to me. I am even beginning to think that one day the presence of Mommy and her "also-ness" might even evoke the same visceral reaction in the family as that of Tatty!

The point is that we need to take stock of how people feel about their interactions with us. We need to think about what energies we are actually giving off, rather than what energies we think we are giving off. It isn't always easy to do this, but it is crucial. The good news is that the *Ribbono Shel Olam* assures us that a small move in the right direction will open up worlds of opportunities for us, as it states, "Open up for Me an opening the size of the eye of a needle and I will open up for you an opening the size of a huge hall."

Consider what energies we are actually giving off, not what energies we think we are giving off.

A conversation with Shelley, today a highly competent psychotherapist, reconfirmed for me an incontrovertible fact of human nature. Shelley related that in her early adulthood and after she got married, she went through a profound emotional crisis, to the point where she felt that she was tottering on the edge. She confided that it was the intervention of my late brother-in-law, Reb Shlomo, z"l, the Rebbe of Denver, who saved her life.

It is said that a sad soul can kill a person more quickly than a germ — and Shelley was the proverbial sad soul. Her extensive training and credentials were unable to quiet the raging demons with which she struggled. At her lowest moment, she claimed, the Almighty orchestrated a "chance encounter" for her with Reb Shlomo. She heard him speak publicly, and when she later sought him out, she felt that with his penetrating gaze, he could see straight into her soul. It was clear to her in that moment that he understood what many years of therapy had not yet uncovered.

From that time onward, Reb Shlomo, as busy as he was, welcomed her calls and accompanied her soul on its journey. His incredibly deep insights gave her the direction she so desperately needed and set her on a healthy path.

Confirming an ancient truth, Shelley stated with great emotion that what affected her most was the fact that a man of Reb Shlomo's stature deemed her worthy of his precious time and input. She felt affirmed and valued, and it was this affirmation that launched her on a productive and successful career as a psychotherapist.

The power of another person's belief in us is conveyed in the Torah's account of Yosef and his close call with the wife of Potiphar. We are told that at the very last moment, the image of his saintly father, Yaakov Avinu, appeared to him, giving him the supernatural strength to withstand the advances of his master's wife — a restraint that conferred upon him for all eternity the designation "Yosef HaTzaddik."

My husband recently observed that *Chazal's* phrase "the image of his father" can be understood on another level. Yosef saw the image of the father he loved, treasured, and respected — but he also saw the *image that his father had of him*, and he could not disappoint him. All during his formative years, Yosef felt the extraordinary faith that Yaakov had in his integrity and his piety. As a result, even the greatest physical temptation in the most pernicious environment could not induce him to betray his father's confidence in him.

Our Sages explain that Aharon HaKohen's unusual talent for influencing even the most alienated Jews was rooted in this same dynamic. He is described as *"ohev es habriyos u'mekarvan laTorah,"* one who loved people and drew them to Torah observance. Experiencing his genuine affection for them, people reasoned that if Aharon HaKohen deemed them worthy of his attention and concern, they must indeed be valuable human beings.

In modern times, my father-in-law, the Hornosteipler Rebbe, Rabbi Yaakov Yisroel Twerski, *zt"l*, exemplified this trait. Years ago, the leader of a modest-sized chassidic community had heard about the extraordinary esteem in which my father-in law was held by his community. Curious as to how this was accomplished, he visited Milwaukee to observe for himself and confirm firsthand what he had heard. After ascertaining that it was indeed true, he approached my father-in-law and asked if he would share with him the "secret formula" of his success.

> *Loving and caring about someone makes them feel taller and more significant. It makes them realize they have great merit. What greater gift can we give others?*

My father-in-law explained that while his community consisted of Jews of all stripes and backgrounds — Holocaust survivors, American-born citizens, immigrants, those committed to Torah and mitzvos, as well as some who were total strangers to religion or had lapsed in their observance — the common denominator was that he loved them all.

The aspiring Rebbe was delighted and thanked my father-in-law for sharing his secret.

Sensing that the young tzaddik had missed the point, my father-in-law stopped him and said, "I can see that you don't understand. What I shared with you, my friend, is not a technique to use as one might wield an instrument. I really *do* love every person I encounter."

In truth, this was the key to my father-in-law's greatness. His was a pure and genuine love.

The love my father-in-law extended to everyone left them feeling embraced by something eternal that was larger than life and would never die. By association, it made them feel taller and more significant. If a person of the caliber of my father-in-law could love them, it must mean that they had merit; this was the greatest gift possible. Indeed, there is no greater gift that any of us can bestow upon our fellow human beings.

Indeed, a wise man once said, "The greatest good you can do for another is not to share your riches with him, but to reveal to him his own." In interacting with others — our spouses, children, friends, and colleagues — it is vital to understand what a difference a good word, a smile, a bit of encouragement, or an expression of concern can make in their lives. Showing love, caring, and giving off positive energy can literally change a person's day — and life.

Stop for a moment and think of your own history. Who has affected you the most? How did they feel about you and how did that affect you? What did that person say to you or give you that somehow made it possible for you to surmount an obstacle, make it through a dark time, or push forward to achieve your goals?

We were enjoying a stimulating Shabbos meal when the topic of "*b'tzedek tishpot amisecha*" came up. This is the Torah obligation to judge people charitably and to exercise great caution before coming to a critical conclusion.

After some of our guests had volunteered their own experiences with this mitzvah, it became clear that Moshe, one of the more animated participants, had fallen silent. We wondered what had affected him so deeply and waited respectfully for his comments.

Finally, he told us that for many years, he and a group of friends who davened in a small Brooklyn *beis hamedrash* had judged another member of the *minyan* as "strange." Yossel, an older man originally from Hungary, was a Holocaust survivor who had a penchant for wisecracking and whose jokes were often tasteless. Over time, Moshe and the other *mispallelim* began to avoid sitting next to him at *simchahs* and other communal events so that they would not be subjected to Yossel's ceaseless barrage of sarcastic barbs. Furthermore, Moshe often made uncomplimentary remarks about Yossel's eccentric behavior.

This went on for many years, until one day, having sensed that Moshe purposely avoided him, Yossel confronted Moshe directly. Moshe felt compelled to tell him that the other members of the shul were very uncomfortable with Yossel's peculiar compulsion.

Yossel invited Moshe to sit down with him for a few minutes. He explained that he was the only survivor of a large family. His parents, siblings, wife, and children had all been slaughtered by the Nazis, *ym"s*, many of them in front of his eyes. These unspeakably brutal images had been seared into his mind and never left his consciousness, even for a moment. So, Yossel continued, though he knew that everyone took him for a fool because of his relentless joking, he nonetheless felt driven to block out these memories, which gave him no peace. He hoped Moshe could understand that making people laugh, even with tasteless jokes, was his only escape from the pictures that haunted him constantly.

Moshe told us how humbled he was by this revelation. He concluded that no one can ever climb into another person's mind and heart; no one can understand how someone else perceives reality. The lens through which each person views the world is absolutely unique.

This leads to a powerful realization. We've seen how we need to be aware of the energies we emit. With the story of Moshe and Yossel, we learn that we need to be understanding of the "negative" energies that others may be giving off as well.

Being on the receiving end of negativity — almost always based on warped perceptions — can be painful and difficult to tolerate.

Sheri was a case in point. Her mother was a person whom everyone found endearing — except Sheri. For reasons she could not fathom, her relationship with her mother was almost entirely negative; her mother was critical, demanding, and nearly impossible to please. Sheri had lost a sibling when she was very young, and it seemed likely that her mother, on a subliminal level, resented her for being the one who had survived. This particular warp is a well-known psychological phenomenon in which people begrudge themselves, and at times others, the gift of life that was denied to loved ones.

This insight helped Sheri see her mother in a different light. While not justifying her mother's behavior, she now was able to see her as a tortured human being trying to make sense of an excruciating blow. Most importantly, Sheri realized that she had done nothing to deserve this treatment and that it was a reflection of her mother's own limitations. It helped her to consider that just as one would not expect a cripple to rise from his wheelchair and walk normally, so too is it unrealistic to expect a person who is emotionally crippled to respond normally.

Psychologists have recently identified a new syndrome called childhood emotional neglect (CEN), in which a child's concerns and feelings are not validated when he or she is growing up, and the child is in essence marginalized, not seen, understood, or valued. The effect is that such children process reality very differently than others, and as adults they make decisions and choices based on these (faulty) perceptions.

Appreciating that human beings have individual realities can give us pause when we are tempted to jump to conclusions or assess them based on our own perceptions.

Malka, an accomplished professional with a beautiful family, once invited Alice, an attractive woman and an influential community member, to come for a Shabbos *seudah*. Alice had just remarried and seemed very happy; during the meal she spoke about the inroads she had made in her field, prompting a twinge of envy in her hostess. By comparison, Malka viewed herself as a slightly overweight mother who had so many responsibilities that she had little time to take care of herself or invest in her career.

In a phone conversation after Shabbos, Malka noticed that Alice seemed to be breathing laboriously and asked her if she was feeling well — or if she had perhaps caught her in the middle of a work-out. Alice's response shook her to the core. She said she was struggling to lift her severely handicapped child into a wheelchair, completely altering Malka's vision of a self-indulgent woman blessed with great good fortune.

Malka came to realize that people are doing the best they can with the resources available to them. If others fall short of our expectations, we need to cut them some slack. Often — usually — they are busy with their own struggles, doing all they can to keep their heads above water.

The Mishnah in *Pirkei Avos* advises, "Do not judge your friend until you come to his place." Since it is impossible to actually take another person's place and experience his situation for ourselves, this means that we are always prohibited from judging others critically. In fact, if we actually understood their "place," we would never want to deal with their challenges. As the Talmud teaches, the *Ribbono Shel Olam* "packs our bags" before we arrive in this world, and we have the resources to handle only what is in our own bags.

Each person gives off different energies. Our job is to change ourselves to give off positive energy and to avoid judging others when they don't.

Debbie, a happily married young woman with a beautiful family, sat in my living room engaged in conversation with one of my Shabbos guests. Suddenly, for no apparent reason, she dissolved into tears and left the room. I followed her out.

She shared with me that the other woman, a recent convert to Judaism, had launched into disparaging remarks about the Christian community in which she had lived before her conversion. Debbie said she had been reminded of her own spiritual journey, during which she had been involved briefly with a group of caring, nurturing evangelical Christians.

She had grown up in a Reform Jewish family that had offered her only minimal information about her religious heritage. When Debbie asked questions about her faith, she had been directed to her parents' "rabbis," who were dismissive and evasive, leaving her frustrated and empty. Disheartened, she was an open target for the Born-Again evangelical movement on her college campus. Vulnerable and thirsty for a meaningful connection to G-d, she was drawn into a warm and supportive circle of fervent believers in Christianity.

Debbie described her experience as a loving one; she said that the members were attentive and concerned for her well-being every step of the way. For example, they always waited up at night to make sure she arrived home safely from wherever she had been. Fortunately, however, Debbie was able to look beyond their warmth and recognize that there was no truth to their beliefs. Eventually, she found her way back to her Jewish roots, but she could not shake her sense of gratitude for what they had given her when she was down and out. Hearing disparaging remarks about them, even years later, was painful to her.

Unquestionably, for a human being, emotional nurturing trumps almost everything else life has to offer. I recently heard an analyst comment that empathy and compassion are on the decline in America and narcissism is on the rise. In part, he faulted what he called "compassion fatigue," which results when the media inundates us with images of horrific occurrences and multitudes of suffering victims. He also cited the encroachment of the Internet, which captures our time and attention and minimizes our involvement in meaningful relationships.

Commentators are shocked by the thousands of Westerners joining ISIS. While there are many reasons for the phenomenon, one cause is simply that young people are looking to belong to a group that will give them a sense of purpose. Perhaps even more importantly, it suggests, ISIS offers a nurturing, close-knit group of individuals who support each other.

The length to which people will go to feel a sense of belonging is mind-boggling. Clearly, while civilization has progressed technologically and in every field of endeavor, the deep inner needs that drive human behavior remain unchanged.

The good news, according to the analyst, is that despite the decline of empathic behavior, human beings are wired for empathy and compassion. To cultivate them, he made the following suggestions:

1. Adopt an attitude of curiosity about others who are not exactly like you.
2. Develop empathic listening skills.
3. Listen for feelings behind the words.
4. Listen to the needs expressed. You can do this by reflecting back to the person what you heard him say. He will feel heard, engendering a meaningful connection that is crucial for conflict resolution.
5. Make use of what psychologists refer to as "contact theory," which posits that bringing people together physically (i.e., giving a hug) breaks down barriers and enables connection and compassion.

It never ceases to amaze me that psychological insights that are considered new and revolutionary have long been part of Torah tradition. My husband once noted a similar concept in the narrative of Yosef and his brothers. The Torah tells us that Yaakov Avinu sends Yosef to seek out his brothers and inquire about their welfare. When he finally finds them, the verse states, "They saw him from a distance, and before he came close to them, they conspired to put him to death."

From the perspective of "contact theory," we understand that as long as the brothers saw him from afar, "from a distance," they could unleash a hateful plan. Where people are not in personal contact, evil gains a footing; when we interact closely with people we have maligned from afar, the dynamics often change, and empathy becomes a stronger possibility.

One of our foremost priorities should be the creation of a sense of family beyond ourselves, enabling people to feel that they belong to one another. As someone once aptly observed, "Family is a haven in a heartless world."

In the absence of a warm and loving family and community and a sense of purpose, Debbie and others like her often make unfortunate choices in their desperation to find a haven. Many young people in our increasingly heartless world make the catastrophic choice to join the most virulent groups in an effort to assuage their dire need to belong and have a mission in life.

It behooves all of us to take stock of our lives — to take a break from the world of distraction and self-indulgence in order to focus on our values, priorities, and relationships. We must find the strength to repudiate the deadly cultural tides that consume us and erode our sensitivity to all that is sacred. We must focus on creating environments driven by empathy and compassion, those that genuinely qualify as family enclaves.

We must increase the love, caring, attention, and sense of belonging and purpose that we show others; we must give off positive energy as much as possible. Every human being deserves it. Every human being needs it.

CHAPTER 3

Attitude

My dear friend, Beth, was recently diagnosed with a life-threatening illness. Despite our closeness, it was a while before she was able to pick up the phone (she lives at a considerable distance) to talk about it. Predictably, as the conversation proceeded I began to cry, and soon we were both in tears.

Reflecting on our talk, I realized that her difficulty in apprising me of her diagnosis was that Beth has always been the bearer of good news. She has, at all times, viewed everything in her life as a blessing — despite the many occurrences and aspects of her existence that could have been experienced otherwise, Beth has always chosen the high road.

In fact, in the midst of lamenting her current condition and the toll it was exacting on her body, she related that shortly before picking up the phone to call me she'd stepped outdoors for a moment. Witnessing the panoramic splendor of the beautiful day, with its blue skies overhead and the ocean sparkling with reflections of the sun's rays, she had choked up and thanked the Almighty for His abundant bounty, the blessings of the past, and most importantly, for the gift of that very moment. Moved by her remarkable presence of mind, I assured her that the Master of the World had certainly made a very wise investment when He chose to give her years filled with what she has perceived as good fortune, because she always responds with gratitude and appreciation. In my humble opinion, I told her, I would think that Hashem would definitely want her continued presence in the world because of the positive energy she brings to it.

I was struck by the startling contrast of the attitude of the inspirational "Beths" in our midst with that of "Korach and his assembly." Korach, *Chazal* inform us, was a person of great stature, a formidable Torah scholar who was brilliant, extremely wealthy, and highly respected. Objectively speaking, he had it all. Nevertheless, he chose to focus on what he *didn't* have. He wanted to be the *Kohen Gadol* instead of Aharon, Moshe Rabbeinu's brother. With his massive font of knowledge and compelling charisma, he convinced some of the greatest leaders of *Klal Yisrael* that Moshe Rabbeinu was guilty of nepotism in appointing his brother Aharon to serve in Israel's highest religious office. Hatred and envy, our Sages state, twist a person's ability to see things straight.

Indeed, Moshe Rabbeinu appealed to Korach and his entourage and said, "Is it insufficient for you, sons of the Levite tribe, that Hashem has distinguished you amongst the congregation of Israel to devote yourselves to Him through your service in the *Mishkan*? Must you also covet the High Priesthood?"

The lesson of Korach's terribly misguided play for power (and its tragic consequences) is relevant for all of us to contemplate. It invites us to scrutinize our own lives and ask ourselves some probing questions, the primary one being: Do we recognize that the life we have, with all of its blessings and challenges, is the life we were *meant* to have, ordained for us by Hashem in His infinite wisdom? Unquestionably, if we could internalize this understanding, we would not waste precious energy on desires and ambitions that don't belong to us, or on making plans that are irrelevant to the unique purpose for which we were created. We would be able to devote ourselves to bringing excellence to that which we do best, and to celebrate the role Hashem has specifically tailored for our individual needs.

> *The life we have, with all of its blessings and challenges, is the life we were meant to have, ordained for us by Hashem in His infinite wisdom.*

"Do not stray after your heart and after your eyes," we say in the daily *Shema* prayer. The obvious question is asked as to why the heart is mentioned before the eyes. One would think that the heart naturally follows the urging of the eyes, *after* they see something desirable.

The commentators explain the sequence by noting that the way we view things with our eyes invariably follows the heart's agenda. In other words, the promptings of the heart, its cravings and its biases, shape and form how we see our world.

Throughout her life, Beth has desired nothing other than what she has, and has consequently seen her life as an endless series of blessings. By contrast, Korach, and his many twisted heirs throughout history, despite their privileged circumstances are conflicted and tortured by desires that they cannot fulfill, and hence cannot appreciate what they already possess.

May Hashem bless us with the wherewithal to open up our hearts to the realization of the wealth of our individual blessings, and our eyes to their presence, moment-to-moment, in our daily lives.

Marsha is an attractive young woman who, despite her many gifts and talents, maintains a posture and attitude of deprivation. She views everything that others possess with an envious and jaundiced eye. In her estimation, life has not been kind to her, and she begrudges the good fortune of others as though their successes determine her failures. Initially, people gravitate toward her, finding her personality appealing. Over time, however, the negative energy produced by her jealousy and general dissatisfaction with life drives them away. At best, she ends up surrounded by malcontents like herself.

My brother-in-law, Rabbi Shlomo Twerski, *z"l*, once offered the following insightful comment. In *Parshas Re'eh* there are two verses in close proximity that appear to contradict each other:

- The first states, "There will not be *becha* (in you) a poor person."
- The second verse reads, "There will never cease to be a poor person *b'kerev ha'aretz* (in the midst of the land)."

Which is it? Will there be poor people or not?

He reconciled the apparent contradiction by drawing our attention to the key words that distinguish the two verses.

In the first verse, a blessing that we will not suffer from poverty, the critical word is *"becha,"* in you. The implication is that if a person looks within himself, from the inside out, he will find the richness of his being. His life will be informed by the treasures that reside within his person. The specific circumstances of his life, whether he possesses much or little, will be incidental and peripheral to his existence. His joy and appreciation of life will come from within.

In stark contrast, the second verse uses the words *"b'kerev ha'aretz,"* in the midst of the land, pointing to the fact that the impoverished person finds himself in this state of being because his point of reference is outward, society at large. He compares himself and what he has (or doesn't have) to external criteria — by what others possess. The perceived good fortune of those around him determines his state of joy, satisfaction with life or lack thereof. He is in a constant competitive mode with everyone and everything around him. This generates feelings of envy and jealousy. It deprives him of an appreciation of the abundance life can offer if only he would look inward for the treasures that are unique to him.

One who looks inside of himself for a definition of his life is wealthy, and he feels it. One who checks his status compared to others is poor, and he feels it as well.

Hence, there is actually no contradiction between the two verses:

- The first refers to the individual who looks inside of himself for a definition of his life. He is wealthy, and he feels it.
- The second is constantly glancing over his shoulder, checking on the status and context of others around him to determine the value of his existence. He is poor, and he feels it too.

Marsha is a perfect example of someone who pursues the misguided approach of thinking that what others have is relevant to us. For starters, this attitude flies in the face of the basic principle of faith that Hashem gives us what we need for the fulfillment of our *tachlis* (purpose) in life. Moreover, and perhaps more importantly, on a day-to-day basis, it drains our ability to relish the many blessings with which we are surrounded. This focus on externals can blind us to what exists *"becha,"* in our own treasure house.

To this end, I have recommended a consciousness-raising exercise that I find helpful. On Friday nights, when we usher in the Shabbos with the lighting of the candles, women traditionally pray for the well-being of their loved ones. In addition to the many requests on our own behalf as well as our children and friends, I importune Hashem to not only bless me and mine, but also to help me appreciate the many blessings with which he has already gifted me. I do not wish to fall into the "Marsha" trap and focus on the darkness, even though it exists in all of our lives. I don't want the brilliance of the sun to elude me. I recognize my G-d-given power to create the energy that will shape the context of the lives of all entrusted to me and those whose lives I touch. And I pray for Hashem's assistance that I remain mindful not of the *"b'kerev ha'aretz"* approach but of the *"becha"* outlook for the coming week.

When the plane landed upon our return from a recent teaching trip, the pilot announced that he had both good news and bad news:

- The good news was that we had arrived early, well ahead of schedule.
- The bad news was that we had arrived early, well ahead of schedule.

He explained that our early arrival, desirable as it was, meant that there was no gate available at which to disembark. We would have to wait almost half an hour to be let off the plane.

The observation that a given situation can be simultaneously good and bad brought to mind the *korban tamid*, the daily offering that was brought in the Holy Temple every morning and evening without fail. Even on Shabbos and *Yom Tov*, when *Musaf* offerings were added for the special occasion, the daily *tamid* came first, preempting all the others.

At first glance this seems counterintuitive. One would think that the sacrifices of the special holiday would be given priority over those that are "routine." Weighing in on this practice, however, the commentators explain that the lesson to be derived is that a person needs to value and appreciate, first and foremost, that which is consistent and regular.

One would think that the special offerings would be given priority over those that are "routine" — but they aren't.

But there is a pitfall. Rav Yosef Salant, *zt"l*, cautions that when something is done daily, it eventually comes to be done by rote, its performance automatic and stale. Rabbi Frand, *shlita*, once cited the example of a bar mitzvah boy putting on tefillin for the first time. How very exciting and heartwarming is this milestone event for him, his parents, and his relatives! Subsequently, though, when it turns into a *tamid*, a recurrent feature of his life, it becomes routine and is taken for granted.

Unquestionably, there is an unfortunate tendency on the part of all human beings to treat whatever is done regularly with a cavalier attitude.

Consider a few examples:

- Tammy, who with great pain lamented the fact that her husband seldom noticed her herculean efforts to provide a pleasant environment for him — a put-together spouse, a clean and neat home, a delicious dinner, etc. — efforts that because of their consistency he had come to expect. To her chagrin, she felt that not only did he fail to acknowledge her hard work or give her positive feedback, he wasn't even aware of the extent of her efforts at maintaining the status quo.
- A similar case was David, whose wife Sarah was threatening to leave the marriage because of what she saw as a lack of emotional nurturing from her husband. When confronted with this criticism, David admitted this shortcoming and avowed that he would work harder to meet her legitimate need. Sarah, on the other hand, had to be reminded that she too had overlooked the fact that David was a good provider and worked long, hard hours to give her that which she had come to take for granted.
- Another not uncommon scenario is that of Aaron, a recent widower who shared sadly that since his wife's passing it has been the seemingly "little things" that bring him to tears. He could not believe that something as insignificant as unloading the dishwasher could set him off. Aaron explained that it was his wife's routine contributions, her *"korban tamid"* for the sake of the marriage that he had failed to appreciate sufficiently.

To paraphrase the pilot's words, consistency has the potential to be both good news and bad news:

- Good news, because the occasional flashes and shimmer of something new, as exciting as they may be, cannot compete in value with the dependable staples of our daily existence. The *korban tamid* exhorts us to open our eyes to the ongoing gifts and blessings that surround us every day, such as our loved ones and our interpersonal relationships.
- At the same time, we need to be vigilant of the bad news, the

tendency to walk mindlessly and "routinely" among daily miracles, oblivious to the wonderful blessings that Hashem lavishes upon us.

It is noteworthy that in our daily prayers, specifically in the *Birchos Hashachar,* we thank Hashem for our ability to see, *"pokei'ach ivrim"* (Who gives sight to the blind). Shortly thereafter, we recite a seemingly redundant blessing, "Who removes the sleep from my eyes and slumber from my eyelids." How many blessings about sight do we really need?

The commentaries provide us with a profound explanation: In the first *berachah,* we thank Hashem for our physical *sight,* the ability to see. In the second, we thank Hashem for *insight,* for the ability to register that which we see and allow it to transform our lives, if we so choose.

Surrounded by so much moment-to-moment goodness in our daily lives, the challenge is to have the good sense to remove our blinders and gratefully celebrate our blessings. We must be extremely cautious not to succumb to the pitfall of sight without insight, i.e., the danger of allowing G-d's daily offerings in *our* lives to be taken for granted.

My daughter Chagi, a multi-talented and exceedingly bright young woman, has managed with great self-sacrifice to be a stay-at-home mother and tend exclusively to the needs of her household. Predictably, there are moments of insecurity when she questions her resolve. My input then is to reassure her that there is a season for everything, and that in the long run, she will not regret having devoted herself to her family in its formative years.

Chagi recently called to give me an update on the success of her domestic venture. She related that on a regular basis, the mothers in her close-knit community who work outside the home ask her to take their children off the bus and keep an eye on them if they happen to be running late. Typically, her house is teeming with action, a haven for the "latchkey" kids in the neighborhood.

Well, one day, her four-year-old, Efraim, came home from school and greeted her with an exasperated, "*Ach*, Mommy, why you '*beez*' home all the time and I never get to go to Duvy's house?"

So much for gratitude, Chagi lamented jokingly.

Another time, she continued her woeful recollections, her daughter Leah'le complained that the other children in her class brought in mitz-vah notes written on napkins and paper plates, while hers were always on pretty stationary embossed with the day of the week.

Here, again, were the thanks she received! Was this, she asked me tongue-in-cheek, a commentary on the success of her stay-at-home career?

In a serious vein, all of us thrive on expressions of gratitude. It was Mark Twain who commented that a single good word or compliment could keep him going for months. Saying thank you is also the most basic sign of *mentchlichkeit*, of being a decent human being.

Mark Twain said that a single compliment
could keep him going for months.

Saying thank you is central to being Jewish. Take a few examples:

- The Jewish People are referred to by the appellation "*Yehudim*," derived from the root word "*hodaah*," meaning thanks.
- Moreover, upon arising every morning and realizing that we have been blessed with another day of life, the first words out of our mouths are "*Modeh Ani*," in which we give thanks to Hashem.
- It is significant that in the repetition of the *Shemoneh Esrei*, the congregation is only obligated to say Amen to each of the *baal tefillah's berachos*. The only exception is the "*Modim*" sec-tion, where we thank Hashem for the gift of life and its many blessings, which every individual must recite on his own. The implicit message is that others may be delegated to represent us in praising Hashem and making our numerous requests, but when it comes to giving thanks we have to do it ourselves.

In fact, the commentaries point out that significant in the "*Modim*" *tefillah* is the passage stating that we thank Hashem for the good that attends our lives "at all times, evening, morning, and afternoon." They suggest that when we recite these words we have in mind three instances of "good" that Hashem has shown us on that particular day. Needless to say, training our minds to have an attitude of gratitude and appreciation for the positive in our lives can be powerful and even life-altering.

Studies have proven, time and again, that an "attitude of gratitude" has not only psychological and mental health benefits, but physical ones as well.

Our niece, Mimi Lowenbraun, *z"l*, (who, unfortunately, passed away recently) is a wonderful case in point. She was a remarkable individual on so many levels. Everyone who knew her recognized her many exemplary qualities, yet few were aware of the pain she suffered for some fifty years because her positive, life-affirming attitude kept her pain under wraps. At the shivah, one person said, "Miriam was a thinker, an initiator, and a sage spokesperson for children, disenfranchised teens, struggling parents and isolated singles. She was one of the finest human beings I've ever met." Another person said, "She was a woman of wisdom, strength, courage, depth, and independence. She toed no line but that of the Almighty. She was honest, open, and strong in all her ways, but always with kindness, love, and a deep tolerance of human frailty and weakness."

Struck at the young age of eighteen with a terminal illness, *r"l*, the doctors gave her no more than six months to live. With Hashem's help, Mimi defied their prognosis and lived fifty more years. Her journey was repeatedly fraught with debilitating health issues, but she always remained conscious, aware, and grateful for the gift of life in the moment. She could easily and justifiably have complained about her compromised mobility, and the huge, swollen leg she had to drag around with great discomfort. Instead, she was grateful for her husband, children, grandchildren, friends, and the wherewithal, despite her limitations, to do *avodas hakodesh* at her husband's side. She was a living example of "*Yehudi*," "*Modim*," and "*Modeh ani*." I think it is fair to say that it was this attitude of thankfulness that prevailed upon the Master of the World to grace us with her exalted presence for this extended period of time. Her inspiring and heartwarming presence will always serve as a living text. We are truly thankful for the privilege of having had her in our midst for sixty-seven years, although we desperately wanted more.

The humorous comments of our youngsters, Efraim and Leah'le, are entertaining and brighten the serious landscape of our daily existence. The hope, though, is that as they grow into adults, their perceptions and understanding, along with ours, will mature into ones that more closely approximate those of the Mimi Lowenbrauns in our midst.

I recently treated myself to an unusual experience. I was dealing with a lot of "stuff" so I decided to take a break and go visit my daughter and grandchildren in Israel. It was a spur-of-the-moment decision and not an easy one. It required leaving my husband for almost two weeks, which is not something I relish. I made arrangements (such as meals) for his well-being. (I kept remembering what a friend of ours said when approached by a life insurance salesman who had offered him a very expensive policy with extraordinary benefits for his wife, should anything G-d forbid happen to him. Our friend's response was, "I want my wife to be comfortable but I didn't say I want her to be happy." I, too, wanted my husband to be cared for in my absence, but not happy to the extent that he wouldn't miss me!)

> *I wanted my husband to be cared for in my*
> *absence, but not happy to the extent that he*
> *wouldn't miss me!*

Typically, my travels are for *simchahs*, speaking engagements, or obligations of different sorts. This time it was purely for personal pleasure. There were no commitments or demands on my time. Nobody knew I was coming or that I was even there; I was able to be totally present with my daughter and her family. Since I am an early riser, I was able to have quality time with my two adorable grandchildren — reading to them and listening to their delightful chatter, undistracted. It was a special treat for me. Ordinarily, like most people, my mind is scattered, going between the past and the future, and in the process the present all but eludes me.

In a contemplative moment, I was struck by how challenging it is to be present in current times. Technology — emails and cell phones in particular — helpful as they might be, have robbed us of centered-ness, of being "in the zone" in any given activity or interaction. This is unfortunate because the level of satisfaction derived from many experiences is a function of how much one is fully engaged, immersed in the flow of the moment. It is difficult to enjoy any event or activity, especially a conversation, if one's mind has meandered away from what is happening to disconnected thoughts about the past and the future.

Psychologists have concluded that the more time spent mentally absent from one's immediate environment and experience, the less happy one feels.

A Harvard study shows that we spend forty-seven percent of our waking hours thinking about something other than what we are doing at the time. This has its uses, of course, when planning a trip, a wedding, a business strategy, or recalling important information and pleasant thoughts from the past. Under those circumstances, staying present-focused is not helpful. Still, if this sort of mental activity becomes one's default mode of thinking, diminished life-satisfaction usually follows. "Mental time travel," as one psychologist calls it, is usually thinking that is riddled with worry, regret, and other unpleasant emotions.

The more we are present, the happier we are.

The wandering mind has been shown to be the cause of great unhappiness. This is actually good news, because we can, if we so choose, train our brain to be more present-centered.

Davening (praying), for instance, is one of the more reliable methods of practicing the art of being present-centered, because if used properly, it serves the same function vis-à-vis the brain as exercise does vis-à-vis the body.

The point is that, while we certainly need to spend some of our time planning for the future and a little bit of our time focused on the past, most of our time should be spent truly living in the present.

Without question, the greatest "present" of all is Shabbos. It is a day that is meant for us to get off the "mad, mad world" of frenzied activities and enter a higher plane of existence. *Chazal* (our Sages) comment that for Shabbos to serve its purpose, our mental attitude needs to be one of considering all matters of the week done and finished ("*melachtecha asuyah*"). We must focus on the day — the present! — and not drag the matters of the past week into this spiritual oasis that Shabbos is meant to be; it would be an unfortunate departure from the spirit of the day. Moreover, we are taught that Hashem, the Master of the World, created for six days and rested on Shabbos; He halted the wheels of activity, the unfolding of the world, and rested.

Similarly, we who are created in His image are called upon to cease and desist from the creative acts of the week and rest on Shabbos. Further, the measure of the human being is determined not only by the creative genius with which G-d has blessed him, but, equally significantly, by his ability (in a G-dlike fashion) to call a halt to that function at will when it is required and necessary.

In this era of exploding technology, it has become painfully obvious that the creative forces, rather than serving us, have actually become our masters. Usage of technology has become insidious, addictive, and ubiquitous. When properly used, this creative force has tremendous potential to benefit mankind; in its unbridled form it threatens our relationships and our souls to their cores.

All of us have experienced the all-too-common scenario in which a carful of people, instead of utilizing their close proximity to interact and relate, are busy on their individual cell phones. All too frequently, I get desperate calls from couples who cite the obsession with computers, iPhones, email retrievals, and the like, as compromising the quality of their time together. Unquestionably, relationships can only thrive in an environment of non-negotiable, undistracted attention to one another. Technology, wandering minds, and lack of focus on the present moment are the nemesis of positive relating, not only with one another but also with one's self.

Consider Sara, who confessed that she was a person riddled with thoughts of worry and anxiety that have compromised the potentially beautiful moments of achievement and fulfillment in her life. The wise counsel she received was "stay out of your mind," shut down the distracting thoughts. The awareness that she could do this allowed her to anchor herself, rather than over thinking and compromising the present moment.

A wise man aptly observed, "Life is available only in the present moment."

And that's where we must go if we want to feel fully alive.

Life is available only in the present moment.

Shloimy, our three-year-old grandson, recently started *cheder*. A few months ago his older siblings were being quizzed on their *parshah* notes at the Shabbos table. In response to Tatty's question as to the name of the week's *parshah*, his older brother Efraim replied that it was "*Lech Lecha*." Little Shloimy, his eyes shining, could not contain his delight and excitedly piped up, "I have *Lech Lecha* at my school too!"

My daughter Chagi knows that one of our greatest pleasures is hearing the *chochmos* of our grandchildren. When she related this anecdote, I couldn't help but think how wonderful it would be if all of us, the more seasoned students of Torah and of life, could feel the same wonder and excitement when viewing things that have unfortunately become "old hat." Sadly, the demands of life often erode the sense of novelty and freshness with which the young address life in such abundance.

Chazal comment on the peculiar construction of the verse relating to the years of Sarah's life. The verse reads: "The years of Sarah were one hundred years, and twenty years, and seven years." Our Sages explain that Sarah's greatness, in large part, consisted of her ability to hold on to the insights and acquisitions of every stage of life and perpetuate them further, such that at the age of one hundred, she maintained the exuberance she had at twenty, and at twenty, she retained the innocent beauty of a seven-year-old. The gift and hallmark of every stage escorted Sarah to the next level and phase of her life. In modern terminology, she did not become jaded or cynical.

Similarly, built into the DNA of every Jew is the wherewithal to be forever young:

- "Yaakov," the name of our third Patriarch, is derived from the root word "*eikev*," meaning a heel, the starting point of the human body. It suggests that if we so choose we can be perpetual beginners, endowed with the ability to muster the enthusiasm and curiosity that generally accompany a new start.
- Conversely, "Esav" is related to "*asuy*," completed and done, a state associated with fixedness and rigidity. It describes someone who has "had it" and has no desire to entertain new possibilities.

Built into the DNA of every Jew is the
wherewithal to be forever young.

It is related that the Kaminker Zeide, an ancestor of my husband, was once sitting at the Shabbos table when he realized he needed a fresh bottle of wine that was stored in the cellar. When he rose to get it, his guests objected to the trouble he was taking and the wear and tear it would exact on his fragile, elderly body. The Rebbe assured them that he would send his *yingaleh*, his little boy, to retrieve the bottle.

Shortly thereafter, the Rebbe returned with the bottle in his hands. The guests inquired as to the whereabouts of the young lad who was supposed to have run the errand. The Rebbe replied that he had indeed called upon the *yingaleh*, but it was the one who resided within himself. He explained that inside each of us is a young child we can access by distancing ourselves from our locked-in "Esav" mentality.

We have all encountered people, who, despite their chronological age, exude a spirit of life and youth. The ability to view life through youthful eyes is a privileged state of being. There is a great emphasis in our tradition that Torah and mitzvos should be "new in your eyes." Indeed, there are many great people in our midst who look at a page in the siddur or verse in the Torah as if they've never laid eyes on them before. It is an attitude toward life — a focus on what we are doing now, right now, and seeing it as something important and new — that is life-changing.

For many of us, when life takes its inevitable toll and our perspective becomes dulled, one of the tools in our toolbox is to call upon the as-yet untarnished *chochmos*, insights, and intuition of our children and grandchildren. Youngsters can serve as wonderful tour guides in a foreign land. They invariably light up with delight as they observe aspects of their surroundings that our busy minds fail to notice. Young children don't know or care that dandelions are considered weeds; to them, they are just beautiful yellow flowers on the lawn. We can all try to enjoy, appreciate, and be present a little bit more.

Children can remind us to be alive!

Consider the following examples:

- Gitty, a professional of note and a spiritually attuned young woman, shared with me that part of her *avodas Hashem* is to take a drive or a walk during the fall season to admire the magnificent changing colors of the leaves. She considers it mandatory, and feels it is almost sinful to pass up the wonders of the Creator of the World.

- Devory sees her challenge as having an appreciative attitude toward the many invitations she receives to weddings, bar mitzvahs, and other *simchahs*. She claims that during "the season" she is simply inundated, and juggling all the festivities with her numerous responsibilities is difficult and overwhelming. She is therefore working on identifying her priorities and limiting her participation in such events in order to be able to sufficiently enjoy and be "present" with a full heart at joyous occasions.

- Ruchi nostalgically recalls the early years of her marriage and wishes to recapture the feeling of "*sameiach tesamach rei'im haahuvim*" of days gone by. There's so much on her plate, she says, that this primary relationship has been put on the proverbial back burner. She and her husband live parallel lives, seldom taking time to connect in a meaningful way. She has therefore resolved to re-engage and invest in this blessing that has somehow come to being taken for granted.

- Finally, there is Chaya, who in recent years has come to dread the *Yomim Tovim*. In her mind, they are associated with hard work and exhaustion, as all her children descend upon her home and every waking moment is spent responding to their needs. We worked on finding a way to help her pace herself, by including others in food preparation, scheduling, and menus. Most importantly, I pointed out that she had to divest herself of the martyr mentality, an occupational hazard for all Jewish wives and mothers. We want to do it all — and then we complain about it. We spoke shortly before Chanukah and Chaya assured me that she would sit on the couch for the halachically-mandated half-hour after candle lighting and simply enjoy the candles' lights. We talked about the glow of the flames and the memories they evoke of our childhoods and the centuries of Jewish history.

The point is that we cannot allow our attitude to life to become jaded, bored, and old. Let us not just be alive. Let's live!

A few weeks ago Tova, an old friend, came to spend Shabbos with us. In the course of the weekend it surfaced that she is a ten-year survivor of breast cancer. As a consequence of her experience, Tova now spends much of her time lecturing and giving encouragement to women undergoing similar challenges. What I found most remarkable about her journey to healing was that at the time of her diagnosis, she was unaware that her particular form of the illness was medically catastrophic, without a smidgen of positivity in the prognosis. Tova attributes her remarkable recovery to not knowing that according to medical research she was supposed to die; hence, she was able to approach her situation with hope and optimism. In fact, she bemoans the fact that doctors today hold nothing back. Playing G-d, they pronounce death sentences upon their patients and deliver hopeless verdicts. Fortunately for her, the days of "Google" had not yet arrived. While she acknowledges that access to online information can be helpful, the downside is that it can wreak havoc with a person's positive attitude.

My brother-in-law, Dr. Abraham Twerski, when speaking about the mind/body connection and the irrefutable power of suggestion, refers to a practice anthropologists discovered among the members of a certain African tribe. In that culture, when someone was found to be guilty of a capital offense, he was not executed by what we would consider conventional means. Rather, an elder of the community would approach the individual with a skeletal bone, which was believed to have certain powers, and point it at him. Within a day or two, without intervention of any kind, the person would be found dead. Such is the power of the mind over the body.

The psychological literature in this area is constantly expanding. We are informed that two areas of gray matter in the brain "light up" when we imagine positive future events. Statistics show that people who expect good things in life are less likely to develop health issues, and more likely to overcome them when they do occur. The good news, according to some researchers, is that we can actually train ourselves to be optimists.

Dr. Huffman, a leader in the field, suggests the following exercise:

Picture your social connections with family members, neighbors, colleagues, and friends; then imagine the best possible future in terms of these relationships five years down the road. Once a week, write about these things in vivid detail for approximately twenty minutes, including how it makes you feel and how you can make it a reality.

Dr. Martin Seligman, in his classic work *Learned Optimism*, suggests that shifting the way we respond to mishaps (and victories) can also strengthen our optimism "muscle." An example he gives (to which I can totally relate) is bafflement in the face of modern technology. A pessimist sees his difficulty in terms of "I'm a moron. I can't do these things, especially since my three-year-old grandchild has no problem with it," whereas an optimist would limit self-criticism to "I'm having an off day" or place the blame on external forces: "These instructions are totally confusing." Interestingly, the way a person reacts to success may also need to be reframed. Instead of attributing success in the kitchen to "luck," the optimist makes a positive affirmation and says, "Wow! I can't believe I'm such a good cook!"

The Torah perspective promotes an attitude of optimism based on faith, trust, and hope:

- Faith is found in the example of the little town where all the inhabitants gather to pray for rain. A lone individual comes prepared with an umbrella. This we call faith.
- Trust is observed in the youngster who is playfully tossed up in the air and dissolves in delight, fully expecting that someone will catch him on the way down. That is trust.
- Hope is when we set our alarm clock upon retiring, despite the fact that no one has promised us that we will wake up in the morning. That is hope.

Of course, we have discussed how mindfulness (being present) and gratitude can help us plug into so much of life that is replete with expressions of optimism, if only we wouldn't take them for granted.

Nachum Ish Gamzu was an inspiring figure in Jewish history. He received his appellation because of his philosophy that everything that happened was for the good. Because of his exalted stature, Reb Nachum was chosen to intercede with the king on behalf of the Jewish People and try to convince him to nullify a catastrophic decree. How?

He was given a chest full of precious stones to present to the king as an expression of the Jews' respect and regard for his leadership. Along the way, a group of thieves robbed him at an inn, substituting dirt for the riches. When Reb Nachum discovered the theft, however, he was nonplussed, still believing that everything G-d does is for the best.

He continued on his journey and presented the king with the chest. Of course, when the king saw its contents he was (predictably) outraged, but his advisors cautioned him not to jump to conclusions. Undoubtedly, they argued, since it came from the Jews, this dirt must have the same magical properties as the dirt their Patriarch Abraham used to overwhelm the armies of the "Four Kings." Sure enough, they sent the chest to the battlefront, threw some dirt at their enemies, and succeeded in gaining the upper hand. Reb Nachum was rewarded handsomely and the decree was averted. The thieves, hearing of the power of the earth with which they had filled the chest, decided to try it out themselves. Predictably, it had no such powers, and they were killed.

Although we may not be able to access the lofty level of faith of Nachum Ish Gamzu, our own modest manifestations of faith, trust, and hope are magnets for good things in our lives.

We are a people of faith. Indeed, having a positive attitude is in our genes. Consider our history:

- We sang *Shirah* at the Red Sea before it split.
- Our grandmothers left Egypt laden with tambourines in anticipation of the miracle, which they then celebrated with song and dance.
- We followed Hashem into an arid desert that was "not cultivated," something that Hashem has never forgotten, as it states, "*Zacharti lach chessed ne'urayich.*" Despite all our lapses,

He always remembers the "kindness of our youth," when we followed Him into the desert on the basis of faith alone.

- Throughout history, despite all the persecution, we have been remarkably successful at living lives of joy.

In the end, we have no control over what happens *to* us, but we have tremendous control over what happens *within* us. It's all in the attitude.

CHAPTER 4

Challenges

T
he *yahrtzeits* of both my parents, *z"l*, came and went in the same month. I was reminded of a passage from a poem:

Though the radiance that was bright
Be forever taken from my sight,
Though nothing can bring back the hour
Of splendor in the grass, of glory in the flower,
We will grieve not, rather find
Strength in what remains behind.

Indeed, my siblings and I find great strength in the remarkable legacy my parents left us.

They were both Holocaust survivors whose world was shattered; their losses were huge. Nonetheless, they came to a foreign land and mustered the strength to rebuild their lives, tapping into the core resilience that we all harbor deep inside.

The necessity of summoning that resilience becomes evident to all of us as we encounter the many challenges of life. This is corroborated by one of the commentaries on the *pasuk* in which Yaakov Avinu asks Hashem, "*V'shavti v'shalom el beis avi*," a request that he be able to return home in a state of peace and wholeness at the conclusion of his journey.

Implicit in this request, the commentators note, is the presumption that there would be bumps along the road, formidable challenges to his spirituality. Therefore, Yaakov appealed for wholeness ("*v'shalom*"), asking that his journey would not exact too great a toll — that at the end of the day, he would not be compromised.

We, too, hope that our greatest achievement will be to conclude our sojourn in this world, with its many blandishments and temptations, only minimally scathed.

Consider Marvin, a major player in the financial arena. By the time he was forty, he was a millionaire many times over. Then the market crashed. He lost his fortune, suffered a heart attack, and soon afterward was diagnosed with cancer. In contrast to the stark fear of everyone in his immediate circle, Marvin radiated a state of calm. He reflected on his life in the fast lane and realized that his trials could be viewed either as a catastrophe or as a wake-up call.

Choosing to withdraw from the "rat race" and the many demands on his life, Marvin was freed to reconnect with his family and to relish the many blessings that had previously escaped his notice. He remarked that the "lenses" through which he now viewed his life enabled him to see more clearly and was thus full of gratitude.

There are many people who choose not to make the huge changes that would take them down a healthier path in life ... and to be fair, such change often requires great strength. It means breaking out of one's habitual behaviors and entering a paradigm shift — an effort clearly not for the fainthearted.

Leah, a highly intelligent woman, was struck with a condition that severely limited her mobility. Her husband saw to it that she had adequate help and tried valiantly to make her surroundings as pleasant as possible. Unfortunately, however, Leah chose to focus exclusively on her limitations, and her husband became increasingly frustrated. Nothing he did seemed to temper her bitterness, and instead of appreciation, she hurled abuse at the hand that fed her. To his credit — and her good fortune — pity for her condition kept him in the marriage.

Certainly, no one has the right to sit in judgment over another person's situation or the way that person meets his or her challenges. Nevertheless, we all have innate resilience, the inherent capacity to rebound, and the wherewithal to *choose* a positive path. And we ourselves are the greatest beneficiaries of that choice.

My parents and many of their generation demonstrated that one *can* rebuild, against all odds and regardless of the circumstances. In this generation as well, we have heroes in our midst whose lives testify to the great courage of choosing to move forward.

---

*One **can** rebuild, regardless of the circumstances and against all odds.*

Yaakov Avinu recognized life's realities and understood that he and his descendants would encounter many pitfalls, both collectively and individually. Thus, he prayed that Hashem would enable him to return home safely — to return a whole person. That *tefillah* is accessible to all of us.

May Hashem give us the wisdom and fortitude to make good use of it.

There are times when the human condition is unbearably painful. A short while ago, my husband and I were called upon to visit a family under siege. This father of young children, and husband of a beautiful young wife, is battling a terrible disease from which Divine intervention will hopefully spare him. Throughout our visit he was grimacing and injecting himself with intravenous pain medication so he could carry on with the visit. His heroic efforts included sharing with us a parable he had come across in his studies, an anecdote about a sculptor who created a magnificent, life-like image of a horse. He placed it in the town square but to his chagrin, nobody stopped to comment on his work. When the sculptor shared his deep disappointment with a friend, the latter explained to him that the horse was so real-looking that everyone assumed it was just another horse. He advised him to cut it in half, thus revealing that it was indeed a sculpture, which would certainly draw people's attention. Only then would they take notice and appreciate his great achievement.

The lesson to be derived, the young man concluded, is that the magnificent functioning of the human body is often taken for granted. It is only when it is taken apart that we stop in our tracks to appreciate the beauty and precision of the gift the *Ribbono Shel Olam* has given us.

Needless to say, I was rendered speechless by the courage and faith of this special young man. I was reminded yet again how many heroes walk among us, and how strong and exalted is the human spirit.

An apropos insight that comes to mind is the explanation of our Sages on the name Rachel Imeinu gave to her son as she was dying in childbirth: *Ben Oni.* The common translation is "son of my pain."

"*Ben oni,*" however, can also be understood to mean "child of my strength."

The dual meaning of "*oni,*" pain and strength, is not a coincidence. There is a parallel between the two. Although it may seem counterintuitive, they posit that it is precisely from encountering, experiencing, and then rising above pain and challenge that we emerge strong.

---

*Ben Oni can mean "son of my pain" or "son
of my strength."
These dual meanings are not a coincidence.*

Certainly, none of us would ask for suffering for the sake of strength, but it is safe to say that no one in this world is given a free ride. Unquestionably, adversity does test our mettle and can, if we react well, bring out the best in us. The result is that the "child of my pain" and "child of my strength" can oftentimes be one and the same. This was the lesson that Rachel Imeinu, our mother and the great advocate of our people, taught us.

Some time ago, I was invited to be Scholar in Residence at a four-day event in Bournemouth, England, sponsored by an organization called "In Touch." Two fabulous women, Toby Waltzer and Tzirele Gluck, conceived of the idea of giving mothers of special needs children a four-day respite in a lovely hotel by the sea, where they were treated to delicious meals, massages, *shiurim*, personal counseling, humorous entertainment, and more. Of course, the most important element of the gathering was the spirit of camaraderie that existed among the women, of sharing a common destiny and "being in this together." It was a humbling experience and extremely inspiring to see women, who despite the fact that they have so much on their plates, can still smile and engage life with upbeat and positive attitudes. There was no question that every one of them, each in her own way, had converted the "*oni*" of pain to the "*oni*" of strength.

While all of us have "stuff" to deal with, when we encounter those who are dealing with unspeakably difficult situations, we are jolted. The perfect sculpture of the horse is torn apart and brings us to an appreciation of how beautiful the horse is when it is intact. It gives us perspective, and leaves us in awe of the many unsung heroes who teach us that lesson.

May Hashem hasten the time when He will wipe away the tears from every face.

Our five-year-old great-grandson, Yitzchak Yankele of Yerushalayim, is a budding philosopher. Typically, he lies awake at night contemplating life. On one occasion, he emerged from his bedroom and asked his mother if it was true that one can see Hashem best in the dark.

Yankele's question was, in fact, very insightful. It is precisely in the "dark," in times of challenge and adversity, that we seek to connect with our Heavenly Parent in greater measure. When we are down and out and find ourselves tottering on the edge, we tend to look toward our Source.

A wonderful story is told about Reb Meir of Premishlan, one of the foremost chassidic luminaries. Reb Meir, even at an advanced age, would awaken before dawn and make his way up a steep hill to a stream in which he immersed himself before davening. A group of anti-Semitic hooligans, aware of Reb Meir's daily trek, conspired to hurt the old man and devised a plan: the following morning they would trail the Rebbe and attack him in a secluded area. As planned, they arose early and began to quietly stalk their prey. As they followed him up the hill, however, they found themselves tripping and falling, unable to navigate the rough terrain. Battered and bruised, they waited for the Rebbe to come down, and in reverent disbelief revealed to him their foiled plot, wondering aloud how it was that they, who were young and spry, could not manage what he, an old man, accomplished so effortlessly. His response was simple and profound: "When one is firmly connected Above, one does not fall down below."

> *When one is firmly connected Above, one*
> *does not fall down below.*

Connection to Hashem is what gets us through the dark, cold nights and bumpy roads of life. The knowledge that Hashem is holding our hand throughout the journey gives us the strength to forge ahead.

I often think of my friend Barbara, z"l, who was stricken with a terminal illness at the young age of thirty-six. When I first met her, she looked like the poster girl for the American dream. She was beautiful, bright, well-educated, and financially successful. The doctors who diagnosed her gave her six months to live.

With determination and indomitable will, Barbara defied their predictions and lived for eighteen vigorous years. The last time I saw her she radiated joy and gratitude, and her words to me were a real eye-opener, expressing an attitude I have since encountered among many who have chosen to connect to Hashem "in the dark." For the first thirty-six years of her life, she explained, she had lived on the fast track, caught up in illusory, superficial frivolities. Then a giant shadow crossed her path. Barbara understood that G-d, through the agent of a serious illness, had placed an impediment before her, forcing her to pause and look for purpose and meaning in her existence. Barbara had not been a religious person as such, but she embarked on a more spiritual path. She became a person, she acknowledged, who she never would have become otherwise.

Individually and collectively we struggle with the human condition. The challenge of many in our affluent society is *"vayishman Yeshurun vayivat,"* when the people of Israel become fat with good fortune they kick [become rebellious] (*Devarim* 32:15). In the end, good fortune doesn't always work out to be so "good" for us; it sometimes causes us to lose sight of the goals that are our *raison d'être*, the reason for which we were created. A secular observer of history noted: "The Jews have demonstrated that they can survive persecution. The question is, can they survive freedom?"

Counterintuitive as it may seem, it was during some of our darkest nights that we produced our greatest works: *Tehillim*, Rambam's works, and even the Talmud itself. This confirms the truism that when the physical and the material realms wane, the spiritual realm waxes. History has amply demonstrated that the reverse is also true. When Jews become overly comfortable, assimilation and alienation set in.

As we survey the landscape of *Klal Yisrael* at present, it is hard to escape the feeling that our nation is worn out, depleted, and disheartened by such a long and extended dark night. Jews everywhere are desperately awaiting the dawn of the Messianic era. There are many suggestions as to what might hasten the process of redemption. Consider the following powerful metaphor presented by my husband:

Two yeshiva boys far from home both receive packages of home-baked cookies from their mothers. The first youngster opens his package, sinks his teeth into the chewy, delectable chocolate chip cookies, and gets lost in the flavor, commenting to his friend that no one in the world can match the taste of his mother's cookies.

The second boy opens his package and is overcome by a deep longing for his beloved mother, whom he can see in his mind's eye puttering about the kitchen and painstakingly shaping each cookie, investing it with love and care for her child.

With the first student, the cookie is the focus.

For the second, it is the relationship he has with his mother.

The Almighty offers us many "cookies" — a world filled with beauty and opportunities of all kinds. Too many of us get lost in the "fat" that causes our people to "kick," to become so bloated that our G-dly objective is obscured. Perhaps if in every gift we are offered we could see the loving hand of our benevolent Parent and reconnect with Him, the *geulah* would finally be in sight.

Yankele's observation that Hashem can better be seen in the dark is undeniable. Let us therefore prove to the *Ribbono Shel Olam*, with our efforts toward mindfulness, awareness, and focus, that we can discern His love and presence in our midst. Convinced of our ability to see Him in the daylight, He will banish the "darkness of night" forever, speedily in our days.

"Even if the heavenly gates of prayer are locked, the heavenly gates of tears are never locked" (Talmud *Berachos* 32b).

It is said that "For people of faith there are no questions, and for non-believers, there are no answers." Even in these times of great tragedy and darkness, as we thrash about trying to find our bearings, we know that Hashem runs the world, and in His perfect wisdom and goodness, everything that happens makes perfect sense.

We, however, are mortals with tunnel vision. The joyous ultimate destiny of Hashem's chosen and beloved people eludes us in this state of impenetrable gloom. Our pain, however, is not born of doubt or of questioning of the Master of the World; it is more of the "*vayidom Aharon*" variety ("and Aharon was silent").

The response of Aharon HaKohen to the death of his exalted sons on the day of the consecration of the *Mishkan* has other, perhaps deeper, meanings:

- *"Vayidom"* is also related to the words for "quiet" and "soft," as in *"kol demamah dakah,"* the way that Hashem manifests His presence in our lives.
- It also means "depend," as in *"Dom la'Shem vehischolel lo,"* depend on the L-rd and hope in Him (*Tehillim* 37:7).

More than just suffering in silence, Aharon HaKohen's reaction points to an abiding faith, a deep *knowing* that whatever Hashem does is ultimately the way it has to be, and moves us closer to the final stage of redemption.

Nonetheless, I find myself inconsolable as I write this, with tears staining the pages of my notebook. It seems that for us Jews, faith and acceptance coexist with pain.

I am reminded of my five-year-old granddaughter Malka'leh, who learned in kindergarten about *"gam zu letovah,"* the concept that everything that happens is for the good. Subsequently, she preached this maxim regularly to her siblings, who became increasingly annoyed by her self-righteousness. Lo and behold, one day she fell off her bed and started crying. Her siblings immediately gathered around her and shouted, "What happened to your *'gam zu letovah'*?"

Quickly composing herself she replied, "Even if you say *'gam zu letovah,'* you can still say 'ouch.'" Even at the tender age of five, Malka'leh intuited that there is no contradiction between simultaneously feeling pain and deferring to Hashem's will.

"Even if you say 'gam zu letovah,' you can still say 'ouch.'"

My husband's great-grandfather, Reb Mottele of Hornosteipel, zt"l, suffered the loss of all his *kesavim*, the scholarly manuscripts he had written over a lifetime, in a fire that destroyed his home. After the misfortune, the chassidim observed a deep sadness that cast a pall over their beloved Rebbe. Knowing him to be the consummate man of faith, they waited for an explanation. Sure enough, a short time later he addressed the issue, noting that the first response to a tragedy must always be to register the pain and feel it deeply, for only then can one move on to a meaningful posture of acceptance.

The first response to a tragedy must always be to register the pain and feel it deeply, for only then can one move on to a meaningful posture of acceptance.

This unique capacity to balance pain and acceptance is exemplified by the breaking of the glass under the chuppah. At the height of one of the most joyous occasions in our lives, we deliberately invoke the destruction of the sacred Temple in Jerusalem, which initiated our bitter exile among the nations of the world. Indeed, celebration coupled with pain is our mandate — simultaneously rejoicing in life amidst an exhortation to remember our suffering.

A touching example of this dual dynamic is the response of one of our congregants, a deeply sensitive and thoughtful physician in our community. Some years ago, he heard my husband challenging the congregation in his Shabbos *derashah* to alter something in their lives, however modest, to mark the deaths of the victims of a recent massacre. In the course of his remarks, my husband questioned whether our empathy was so real that it would stop anyone from eating dessert in deference to the loss. Ever since then, Dr. Larry, a frequent guest at our table, has consistently declined his portion of dessert.

At a recent *simchah*, a woman told me about her son who is studying in Israel and was scheduled to return to America for his brother's wedding. After the horrific events of the Har Nof massacre, he called his mother and informed her that his beloved teacher and mentor was one of the victims; he was so grieved that he could not find it within himself to come to the wedding. His mother understood and did not push him. A short time later he called back and said that he had sought the counsel of a *gadol*, who had emphatically urged him to attend the wedding. Moreover, he had insisted that the young man rejoice with his whole heart and soul.

We pause, register the pain, integrate our acceptance of it, and move on to embrace life. This is the Jewish way.

Notwithstanding the above, my heart finds great resonance with a story that is told about the Mirrer *Rosh Yeshiva* and *Mashgiach*, Reb Chaim Shmuelevitz, *zt"l*, who immediately upon arriving in Israel after the Holocaust made his way to Kever Rachel. Standing in front of the curtain by her grave, he noted the inscription from the Book of Jeremiah, where Hashem speaks lovingly to the inconsolable Mama Rachel and comforts her as her children are being driven into exile. "Hold back your voice from crying," He says. "I promise that I will bring them back from the lands of their enemies."

Reading these words, Reb Chaim Shmuelevitz burst into tears. "No, Mama Rachel, don't stop crying!" he said. "Cry! Storm the heavens with your tears. Cry for mercy on behalf of your children before the Throne of Glory. Cry, Mama Rachel, because the gates of tears are never locked, and your tears will surely make our Heavenly Father declare an end to our travails and suffering."

Certainly, terrorism in Israel, as well as the enmity encountered by our people throughout the world, move all of us to second Reb Chaim Shmuelevitz's appeal to Mama Rachel, that she not relent in her continual advocacy for her beloved children.

May *Hashem Yisborach* redeem us speedily in our time.

Consider these two different stories of loss:

- Chani tearfully described to me the last days of the life of her beloved grandmother. Chani had been privileged to be at her bedside during that time, holding her grandmother's hand and expressing heartfelt gratitude to her for many years of nurturing, wisdom, and love. Chani told me that in Bubby's eyes, she could do no wrong. Her grandmother had magnified her every achievement; she had taken great pride in her beautiful family and had been her greatest advocate and cheerleader. Chani could not imagine life without her. After she passed away, Bubby was taken to Eretz Yisrael for burial, and Chani was unable to accompany her parents. On top of that, most of the shivah took place overseas and out of town, leaving Chani feeling that she was never able to grieve properly and thus achieve closure.

• Meira lost her mother about the same time. She had been a devoted and attentive daughter, but because of unforeseen circumstances, she did not make it to the hospital in time to spend her mother's last moments with her. She did, however, join her siblings for the week of shivah. Her children, grandchildren, extended family, and friends all came to pay their respects and share their memories of her mother. The family laughed and cried together as they reconstructed their mother's life anecdotally, assessing the measure of their loss. When it was over, Meira felt that shivah had provided her and her siblings with meaningful comfort, healing, and closure.

Loss and bereavement are among the most painful and difficult passages that we have to navigate in our lives. The fragility of life and our inherent vulnerability are sobering realities that we all must face.

The difference between Chani's unresolved pain and Meira's peaceful resolution of her grief was the ritual of shivah. In its deep wisdom, the Torah recognizes our need to feel supported at a time when we are experiencing an overwhelming sense of diminution and abandonment, and it mandates the shivah call, conveying the message that though the loss is great, we are not alone. A community of family and friends demonstrate that they genuinely care and want to support their suffering loved ones. The shivah states, in no uncertain terms, that a grief-stricken family has not been forsaken.

Moreover, and of even greater significance, when visitors invoke Hashem's Name and presence repeatedly in the *nichum* formula ("*HaMakom yenachem es'chem*") and in Kaddish, we are reminded over and over again that though our hearts ache and our spirits are devastated, our Heavenly Parent has not left us and will never leave us. We are always in His embrace, He is always at our side, and come what may, He orchestrates events for our ultimate benefit.

The Torah states, "You are children of Hashem, your G-d; you shall not mutilate yourself for the dead" (*Devarim* 14:1). This verse prohibits any form of self-injury when one is in a state of grief over the loss of a loved one. The fact that the Torah calls us "children of Hashem" in the context of this prohibition is unmistakable in its import. The Torah is reminding us that even though we feel overwhelmingly alone, even though our familiar landscape has been ripped away and left us in a state of existential crisis, we are nevertheless children of Hashem, and He will always be there for us. Mutilating ourselves, therefore, is not only uncalled for; it is a complete misunderstanding and violation of this fundamental truth.

For those left behind after a death, there is but one enduring source of comfort. Being there for an ailing loved one when it counts, sharing wonderful memories, the consolation of shivah visits, resting in the embrace of our families — all of these things help to dull the pain of bereavement.

However, the supreme balm is our ability to appreciate that under all circumstances we are children of Hashem — that we are brothers and sisters who share a common destiny of *nitzchiyus*, of resurrection, eternity, and ultimate triumph over evil, death, and suffering.

This assurance of our prophets and Sages enables us to navigate the otherwise turbulent storms of life, knowing that He will be with us no matter what happens, accompanying us on the journey to our personal destiny.

Life is full of surprises, some of them of our own making. And not all surprises are fun.

Some time ago, I had an overflow of guests for our Shabbos *seudah*. My ovens in the kitchen were already filled to capacity, and with more food to warm I resorted to an old basement oven that serves as a spare in case of emergency. As I opened the oven door — surprise! — I was greeted by a horrendous stench. The source of this distinctly not-fun surprise was a pan of forgotten food that, as best as I can surmise, must have been sitting there since the *Yom Tov* season many months earlier. It must have been overlooked when I instructed one of my grandchildren to bring up *everything* from the downstairs oven.

I immediately sprayed Easy-Off, a medley of particularly caustic chemicals, on every inch of the oven's interior, then applied every cleanser known to mankind — yet I still could not dispel the offensive odor. I was advised by experts to place a can of coffee granules in the oven, which, they assured me, is *always* effective in absorbing malodorous scents (a nice way of describing the problem). However, all of my efforts were ultimately futile and I raised my hands in surrender, believing that my emergency fallback oven was doomed to become a relic of the past. Until this Purim.

Every Purim, the local yeshiva dispatches busloads of boys to our side of town to join in our *simchas Purim* and to circulate among the *balebatim* of the neighborhood to contribute to the day's merriment. They are a delightful bunch and I look forward to having them at my table. Once again, I was confronted by the logistical challenge of limited oven space versus large crowds of people to feed. In desperation, I prayerfully and reluctantly put the overflow food into the downstairs oven. Lo and behold, a remarkable thing happened. The aroma of the delicious fare canceled out the objectionable problem. The new scent of meatballs, kreplach, and stuffed cabbage achieved what an endless array of chemicals, vinegar, and determined scrubbing could not.

Every occurrence, no matter how mundane, is instructive to the larger picture of our lives, and my foul-smelling oven experience was no exception. What I took away from it was that the best way to deal with the noxious and undesirable occurrences in our lives is not to dwell on them excessively, erroneously believing that in so doing we can extricate ourselves from their hold over us. Rather, the more effective approach is to fill ourselves with positive and light-hearted energy, thereby dispelling the negative forces.

Indeed, we are taught that "a little bit of light banishes a great deal of darkness." One of the chassidic greats promotes this idea by commenting on the counsel of King David in *Tehillim*, "*Sur mei'ra va'asei tov.*" Ordinarily, this translates as "Turn away from evil and do good." The commentator, though, makes a subtle but crucial change, interpreting it to mean "Turn away from the indiscretions and failures." How? "By doing good." This insightful counsel informs us that if we wish to disabuse ourselves of that which is detrimental to us, what we need to do is to break away from our preoccupation with the darkness and immerse ourselves in light.

Consider:

- Emily, who couldn't make it through a conversation without obsessing about her abusive past. The grievances and resentments toward the people who had wronged her were all-consuming; or
- Shaindel, who couldn't let go of guilt feelings emanating from regrettable behaviors in which she had indulged in her younger years; and
- Rivka, who couldn't forgive herself for being what she perceived of as an inattentive daughter to her now deceased mother.

The list is endless and encompasses a litany of memories that hold people in dark and unforgiving dungeons of the mind. We all have challenges. We all make mistakes. While it is true that a "*cheshbon hanefesh*," an assessment of our spiritual health, can certainly be helpful insofar as it is instructive for the future, obsessing about our past shortcomings is ruinous. My father-in-law, *zt"l*, a very wise man, used to say, "There was no event in my life that I consider a failure if I learned from it." Wallowing in the past is invariably counterproductive, if not actively destructive. It robs one of the ability to enjoy and celebrate the blessings of the present.

Failures are not failures if you learn from them.

Over the past half-century, many schools of psychology have abandoned the approach of delving into their clients' often sordid and traumatic histories. Instead, variations of present-oriented therapeutic approaches concentrating on the "here and now" have very successfully replaced the older techniques.

It is fairly clear that all of the scrubbing and laborious efforts to do away with a "malodorous" past are not as effective as simply letting go and filling our lives with bursts of sunshine. Even as there are weeds and thorns in the fields and gardens of the world, there is also an abundance of exquisite and fragrant flowers releasing their scent into the air we breathe. There are brilliant vistas of beauty to enrich our internal environment, our person, and our psyche.

> *Trying to delete the past is not as effective as simply letting go and filling our lives with bursts of sunshine.*

Restoring what appeared to be an oven's compromised function proved to be a powerful metaphor for reclaiming psychological well-being. It is a lesson worth remembering: Life can be hard. We need to let the sunshine in.

CHAPTER 5

Relationships

An essential prerequisite for receiving the Torah (which, according to our Sages, constituted the *kesubah*, the marriage contract between us and Hashem) is the relationship we have with our fellow Jews. In the later years of our history, the days of *sefirah* — preparing us to receive the Torah on Shavuos — came to be a period of mourning, commemorating the death of the students of Rabbi Akiva, who, despite being tremendous scholars, perished because of their failure to accord each other the appropriate respect. Clearly, the timely message is that Hashem will not tolerate a relationship with us if we are at odds with our brothers and sisters, His children.

This is of particular significance to women because we are, simultaneously, both privileged and challenged in this area. Women are relational beings. There are those who suggest that this is because Adam, the first male inhabitant of the universe, came into existence in a world where no one else existed, whereas Chava came on the scene with Adam already present, hence her need, and G-d-given ability, to relate.

Be that as it may, women (as a general rule) are equipped with an intuitive, superior emotional intelligence, qualifying them for their role as primary nurturer of their offspring. Many women have commented that while they suffered many setbacks over the years, the only ones that affected them to their very core were in the realm of interpersonal relationships: divorces, alienation from children, etc.

Women relish friendships to a degree that men can't fathom. For many women, their friends are literally their lifeline, with whom they can share without the need to explain. There is an underlying commonality, an understanding, a natural camaraderie.

Women relish friendships to a degree that men can't fathom.

The caveat, however, is that this trait, as laudable as it can be, is only beneficial within limits. Sharing with friends is wonderful as long as it respects boundaries, doesn't abrogate propriety, and doesn't become *over*-sharing or sharing with the wrong person. Discretion and *seichel* must be exercised under all circumstances to prevent this marvelous capacity from becoming a liability.

Consider the following scenarios:

- Yossi, married only a few months, came into his counseling session obviously distraught. His complaint was unfortunately not an uncommon one. He related that his wife Sarah was a young woman who had come highly recommended. She was bright, caring, well put-together, and had all the qualities that should make for a worthy and suitable mate. But there was one significant issue that prevented them from creating a real bond. Basically, he reported that they seemed to be living parallel lives; he did his thing and she did hers. He didn't feel that she had made the necessary shift from sharing with her girlfriends to sharing with her husband, and he felt that he was being left out in the cold. He did not feel that they had progressed at all in their emotional intimacy. In fact, he felt quite superfluous to her existence. Yes, he did appreciate that she was popular among her friends, but her popularity was too much of a good thing.

- Leah was another case in point. She was a wonderful, giving person who extended herself unselfishly to others, especially to her neighbor Toby, filling in as a babysitter and driving her to appointments. The problem, though, was that she was very needy. She desperately sought an embracing, caring environment in which she might feel part of a family, having grown up in an atmosphere she perceived as cold and unemotional. At first, Toby relished the relationship and all the perks that came along with it. Eventually, however, Toby's husband David complained that Leah's neediness, constant presence, and demand for attention were draining Toby's energy so much that he felt there was precious little left over for him. He pointed out to his wife that we all have a limited amount of emotional strength, and when she did most of her sharing with Leah, their relationship suffered.

Indeed, friendships are critical for the emotional well-being of women. Meeting with friends and sharing girl-talk is therapeutic for most of us, but balance is the key. All things, even good things, when done to excess are detrimental.

It is noteworthy that speech is considered to be the hallmark of a human being. No other species is endowed with the ability to speak. The verse in *Bereishis*, "And He blew into his [Adam's] nostrils a living soul" is rendered by Onkelos to mean that the manifestation of the soul with which Hashem endowed man is his ability to speak. Hence, speech used appropriately is an expression of our *neshamah*. Rabbi Shamshon Refael Hirsch, in his typical style of being a great advocate for women, interprets the comment, "Ten measures of speech were given to mankind, and women took nine of them" as meaning that women have a greater ability to give expression to their soul, to connect spiritually. Detractors, however, jokingly interpret our Sages' statement as indicating a proclivity for useless chatter.

Clearly, both interpretations are possibilities, and the choice is ours. Does speech constitute an invaluable tool for connecting and relating, or do we debase it by using it inappropriately?

It is important to note that one of the great attributes of a loving, self-effacing person is the ability to listen without bias or judgment. My husband, *shlita*, once defined the phenomenon of listening as carving out a space in the mind to make room for what the next person is saying. This, he commented, is no small achievement, because the cacophony of external and internal noises so thoroughly fills our heads that it is difficult to do. Typically, we are so consumed with our own thinking and agendas that deep listening doesn't happen.

This is not only the case in human relationships, he asserted, but also the lament of the Almighty when He pleads with His children (such as in the *haftorah* of *Parshas Masei*) to listen: "*shim'u.*" Our Sages tell us that a Divine call goes out from Mount Sinai every day, urging us to return to our Heavenly Father. Tragically, because of the racket in our heads, this entreaty goes unnoticed.

Listening takes many forms:

- There are superficial auditory sensations, which, as they say, "go in one ear and out the other;"
- There is the kind of listening that is a product of genuine love and caring, where the words actually penetrate the heart.
- True hearing goes beyond what the other person is saying and reads between the lines for what the other person *isn't* saying in so many words.

My friend Beth, who is battling a terrible disease, called me recently to relate that her beloved, six-foot-tall, strapping teenage grandson had come for a visit from out of town. He had known that she was ill but was unprepared for what he saw when he arrived. Upon seeing how ravaged his grandmother was by the disease, he lifted her petite body in his strong arms and rocked her back and forth, all the while convulsed in sobbing. Beth was touched to the core. Her grandson had "heard;" he had understood and intuited in the deepest sense that what his grandmother needed most of all at this point was an expression of his love and the knowledge that she had made a difference in his life. In the most significant way, she felt that her life was vindicated. He had given her the gift of quintessential "listening."

It is fair to say that all of us share a basic need for love and connection. If we could learn how to "listen," we would not only better respond to our spouses, children, parents, friends, and coworkers, but discover how much more connected we become to life itself and enrich our collective world.

The first step is to quiet the "noise" in our heads — the many distractions that drown out the voice of Hashem appealing to us to "come home" to the eternal relationship that gives genuine and enduring purpose to our lives.

A touching anecdote is told about two youngsters who have worked long and hard to build a castle in the sand at the seashore. They are shrieking with glee as their castle gets taller and taller. Suddenly, a huge wave comes along and topples their creation.

The adults, observing the scene, look on with horror as the castle is washed away, fully expecting the children to be heartbroken over their loss. It's only natural, they reason; just look how many adults there are in the world who become depressed when *their* empires are undone by economic downturns or changes in fortune. To their surprise, however, the children merely laughed, grabbed each other's hands, and then sat back down to the business of rebuilding their castles.

One of the adults commented, "I guess if you have someone else's hand to hold, you can deal with anything in life."

The Mishnah teaches that one of the forty-eight ways to acquire Torah is to "help his friend carry his burden." The obvious question is: What does commiserating with a friend have to do with the acquisition of Torah? Quite the contrary, one would think that taking time out to help another person would take away from the hours one has allotted to study Torah!

My husband, *shlita*, shared a beautiful insight. He said that, left to our own devices, there is only a limited amount of Torah a person can acquire on his own. It is only when we connect with another individual and become one with him that his Torah becomes our Torah.

In other words, when we are compassionate (a word derived from the Latin meaning co-suffering), we merge and become one with that person. His achievements become ours, and ours become his. By "holding hands" with another human being, we not only benefit that person but expand our own horizons to include what would be impossible to achieve on our own.

> *By "holding hands" with another human being, we expand our own horizons to include what would be impossible to achieve on our own.*

He further extrapolated that this is at the core of Rashi's explanation of why Yaakov Avinu waited until the end of his life to chastise Reuven. Rashi says that Yaakov was fearful that if he apprised Reuven earlier that he had lost his status as the firstborn, Reuven might have reacted by joining forces with his uncle, the wicked Esav. At first glance it strikes us as rather far-fetched. Yet upon deeper reflection, it makes perfect sense that in his state of disappointment and rejection, Reuven would want to commiserate with Esav, who had suffered a similar loss. Esav, too, was disenfranchised and stripped of his birthright as the eldest. By co-suffering and "holding hands," their souls would have merged and Esav would have become part of Reuven. This was Yaakov Avinu's worst fear. He therefore waited until the end of his life to give Reuven this painful information, as by then he was in a better position to handle it.

The message for all of us is that we need to be super-vigilant about whose hands we hold, figuratively speaking.

Indeed, with whom do we choose to merge? We need to examine the icons and the role models in our lives. We dare not allow the likes of Hollywood stars, sports figures, and depraved individuals and ideas to become part of us and enter our souls.

By the same token, connecting with another human being mitigates existential loneliness and the vicissitudes of life. It behooves us, there-fore, to promote connectedness between people by reaching out and listening to each other with genuine interest in everyday conversation, making sincere inquiries about the well-being of others, and by being present and loving in our relationships. In doing so, with warmth and a smile we can help offset some of the harshness of living in today's world, and we all will be left feeling more whole and equal to the chal-lenges that are set before us.

Someone once aptly observed that the objective of life is not find-ing ourselves, but rather creating ourselves. Who we become over the course of our lives has much to do with how and with whom we choose to "hold hands."

There are many aspects of our daily lives that may not appear to oc-cupy front and center, but are nevertheless of tremendous significance.

This was demonstrated by a phone call I recently received from my daughter Ruchi, *tichyeh*, who lives in Brooklyn. She related that when she tucked her nine-year-old daughter Sarah into bed the pre-vious night, my granddaughter had pointed to an empty space next to her on the pillowcase and told her that its smell reminded her of her Bubby in Milwaukee. Sarah asserted that it helped her relax and fall asleep more easily and have happy dreams. She also asked that her mother exercise caution when laundering the pillowcase so as not to wash away Bubby's fragrance, her sleep aid. How sweet for a grandmother to hear!

What was the connection between the pillowcase and me? And why does that allow her to sleep? A renowned psychologist observed that "Our brain makes sense of the world through associations. We understand things in terms of other things, the essence of metaphor. How does one understand something new? By relating it to something familiar and making a metaphorical association. When the automobile was first introduced, people could hardly fathom what it was and soon began to call it a horseless carriage. The association of the two concepts fostered easy understanding and integration of the new idea."

When the automobile was first introduced,
people could hardly fathom what it was.
Calling it a horseless carriage helped ...

I suspect that on a subconscious level, the space on my granddaughter's pillow carrying the fragrance of her Bubby, who she knows loves her deeply, imbues her with the trust and confidence to let go and allow herself to drift off to sleep. In her mind, Bubby's love for her is a metaphor for the love of Hashem, Who even young children recognize as the ultimate Protector and Source of safety and security.

Without appropriate educational institutions in Milwaukee at the time, my older children were sent to New York at a very young age to board with my parents, z"l. Sending them away from home was a very painful experience for me, but in retrospect they gained so much from the exposure to their phenomenal grandparents and the intimate relationship it fostered. It is amazing that to this day, whenever they merely walk into the entranceway of what used to be Bubby and Zeide's house in Bensonhurst, they are overcome with emotion. The flood of memories is triggered by the olfactory associations, the unique fragrance of this wonderful oasis of their youth. These powerful associations provide a safe place they can visit in their minds and hearts in what is often a turbulent and indifferent world. Their memories allow them to be transported back to a time when life was less complicated, and where they were surrounded by unconditional love.

Some time ago, I facilitated a discussion group of professional single women. I went around the room and asked them to introduce themselves by their Jewish names and share some of their background information, with an emphasis on their mothers and grandmothers. What emerged was truly fascinating. The young women made a distinction between "bubbies" and "grandmothers":

- They identified their grandmothers as products of our culture: competent, efficient, and pragmatic, functioning, in large measure, in the public arena. If they wanted to visit "Grandma," they had to make an appointment. She had a life of her own, and a visit had to fit into her busy schedule.
- By contrast, "Bubby" was always available to them. Moreover (and at this point many of the women's voices cracked and their eyes filled with tears), Bubby always greeted them with great delight, offering them their favorite soup or chocolate chip cookies. They had a sense that they were essential to Bubby's life and that she lived in anticipation of their visits.

For some people, there is a distinction between "bubbies" and "grandmothers."

We all have our own variations of the space on the pillowcase, the aroma of a grandparent's kitchen, or the lingering sweetness of a piece of apple cake served by a loving hand that triggers memories and associations. They gift us with metaphors that enrich and warm our lives. Most importantly, they allow us to project and to believe in the goodness of a Creator Who transcends any mortal pleasure or encounter.

The call from my daughter touched me deeply, reminding me that the small things in life are in reality the big things. It brought to mind the anecdote about the teenager who was asked to name the current heads of state and international political leaders. Prominent as they might be, she couldn't remember any of them. However, when asked if she could recall the name of a past teacher or a favorite aunt, the information flowed effortlessly. When questioned about the disparities in her response, she confessed that the former meant nothing to her. The latter, however, impacted her life with love and caring that would forever stay with her.

The message for all of us is that making a difference in another person's life doesn't require an overhaul of our existence. Our impact is in the small gestures, in being present in our interactions, and in not allowing ourselves to be distracted by lesser concerns.

It's not about the public stage. The best associations and the most meaningful metaphors for living come from the private inner stage of life.

It is an indisputable truth that in life, the little things are often the big things. A good friend underscored this fact to me recently when she related how touched she was to discover a tiny cholesterol pill waiting for her on the breakfast table each morning. She told me that while she has many other reasons to respect her husband, a great *talmid chacham* and communal leader, his mindfulness in placing the pill where she will be reminded to take it every day is, to her, the ultimate symbol of caring and devotion. It tells her, very simply, that her husband thinks about her.

Cynics might claim that this is no big deal, that she is making much out of nothing. After all, it's not exactly in the same league as diamonds, furs, or precious jewels. Nonetheless, I can confirm my friend's sentiments from my own experience and from over fifty years of counseling that emotional nurturing trumps everything in a relationship. Fame and fortune, intelligence, and notoriety predominate in the marketplace, but in relationships, atom-sized symbols carry the greatest magnitude of power. However tiny its size may be, a personal expression of thoughtful attention speaks volumes.

*In relationships, atom-sized symbols carry
the greatest magnitude of power.*

An important cautionary note is in order. Quite frequently, the significant others in our lives — husbands, children, friends, and associates — aren't aware of what truly matters to us. A common refrain heard from couples in distress is, "If he/she really loved me, he/she would automatically know what to do to make me happy. I wouldn't have to tell him/her." As desirable as this would be, the fact remains that it is only a fantasy. It is *our* responsibility, as part of the communication process, to let others know what we value in order to make it possible for them to respond appropriately.

Typically, the essence of the complaint is "It isn't the [cruise/Lexus/yacht/necklace] that I wanted; I just wanted some quality time together." On his part, the core of his grievance is not the absence of pheasant under glass for dinner (although that might not be such a bad idea, on occasion) but the excitement he would like his wife to show about his return home by getting off the phone when he comes through the door after a long day.

The truest expression of emotional intimacy is doing for the other on the other person's terms. This, of course, requires one to take the time to climb out of oneself and his own biases, likes, and dislikes, and search the depths of the other person's psyche, to really "get" the other person and understand what makes him tick.

Some women might scoff at the idea that their husbands could ever be capable of intuiting their emotional needs adequately. The reality, however, is that even men are educable!

Perseverance and patience are the key components. Most important, though, is that when they come through for us we give them positive feedback. It is critical to note as well that when we think the other person isn't rising to the occasion, we should realize that it is usually not for lack of caring, but that for the most part, husbands (men) are clueless. It is alleged that Sigmund Freud, the father of psychology, remarked in frustration on his death bed, "Women! I can't figure out what they want!"

If the "experts" are mystified, what can one expect from ordinary folk? It is therefore incumbent upon us to spell things out clearly in all our relationships, especially the spousal relationship.

A close relative once shared a personal anecdote that illustrates this point very aptly. She recounted that she had always relied on a *halachic* leniency regarding the washing of *negel vasser* upon rising in the morning. Halachically, one is supposed to wash one's hands immediately upon awakening before touching any part of the body or foodstuff. Since there was a sink close to her bed, she had always relied on a ruling of "near proximity" to satisfy this requirement. Her husband, however, always insisted on having a *kvart* of water and a basin right next to his bed so he wouldn't have to step down in order to reach a source of water. Subsequently, she said, she heard a *shiur* where the *rav* spoke of some noteworthy Kabbalistic implications of having *negel vasser* next to the bed, and the benefit of not allowing one's feet to touch the floor before washing one's hands. Disheartened that she had not been advised of this earlier, she admonished her husband, accusing him of deliberately withholding this information so as to avoid sharing his eternity with her — since his rigorous observance would certainly earn him a loftier perch in *Gan Eden* (although she was being facetious, she acknowledged that applying a little Jewish guilt never hurt!). Since that conversation, she says that she has found *negel vasser* next to her bed each morning. All she had to do was register her request.

Many husbands acknowledge that one of the "little things" that make a difference to them is finding their wife attractively attired when they return home after a trying day at work. Quite often, wives decry this as demanding and unreasonable; after all, women also put in long days that are fatiguing and heavy with labor. Why add an additional element of stress?

The justice of this argument notwithstanding, my experience has shown that this is by no means inconsequential:

- The Talmud in *Taanis* records the well-known incident involving the sage Aba Chilkiya, whose wife regularly greeted him upon his return from work in her most dignified and attractive apparel.

- Rebbetzin Weinberg, *a"h*, the wife of Ner Israel's *Rosh Yeshiva*, would counsel *kallahs* and newlyweds to be sure to honor this practice.
- Similarly, when spouses greet each other after the daily separation of work hours, a ready, warm smile is an invaluable and treasured gift.

Aba Chilkiya's wife regularly greeted him upon his return from work in her most dignified and attractive apparel.

My daughter Yocheved often reminisces about her grandmother, my mother, *z"l*. She recalls that when Bubby was in the hospital and it was her turn to stay overnight with her, she stopped in the hospital gift shop to purchase a vase with a single rose. Forever after, Yocheved relates, Bubby referred to the beautiful flower Yocheved had so lovingly bought for her. A relatively small gesture, but so meaningful to any person, especially someone in a vulnerable situation.

After I was struck by a car a number of years ago, my children, family, and friends reached out to me with great affection. They brought food, thoughtful gifts, and manifold expressions of caring. One of the "little things" that meant so much to me during that difficult time was my friend Cissy's appearance every day, no questions asked, saying nothing but simply sitting silently by my bedside or next to my wheelchair doing her knitting. I didn't have to entertain her, I didn't have to talk; she was just there, a comforting balm for my aching and traumatized body and psyche. It was caring on *my* terms, not a projection of her ideas about what I should want, but understanding what would work for me.

Nurturing relationships does not require an overhaul of our lives. Most often, all it takes is what the world might consider a "little thing," but what in the world of the beneficiary, who feels noticed and loved, is a gift of infinite magnitude.

A noted psychologist reported two cases in which he saw positive results:

The first one involved a client who was a Holocaust survivor, who had lost his entire family, a wife and six children, in the death camps. Some years after the liberation, he married a woman who, as it turned out, could not have any children. Heartbroken, he confided in the psychologist that since he had no survivors and no one to say Kaddish for him after his demise, he really had no desire to go on living.

The psychologist suggested that he consider the fact that after 120 years, he would be reunited with his martyred wife and children. The survivor, with tears streaming down his face, responded that he did not believe that to be the case. Inasmuch as his wife and children had died "*al kiddush Hashem*" (Jews who are martyred for the sake of the Divine name), and tradition teaches that people who lose their lives *because* they are Jews are holy and pure and merit the most exalted places in Paradise, he, however, had survived and would undoubtedly be compromised by the inescapable pollutants of life. He therefore would unlikely deserve such a lofty level in Heaven, and as such, he lamented, their paths would probably never cross. The psychologist with great wisdom pointed out that no suffering or tears go unnoticed. He assured the tortured soul before him that his excruciating suffering over his many losses were of equal significance, and that living "*al kiddush Hashem*," infusing life with joy and purpose in the wake of a tragedy of such magnitude, was perhaps even more meritorious. The psychologist was able to get his client to realize that his fears were unfounded, and he could rest assured that he would rejoin his family in eternity.

The second case the psychologist shared was one of a widower who, even with the passage of much time, could not get past grieving for his wife. He could not make sense of his life, and was unable to invest purpose in his lonely, anguished existence. In the course of his therapy, he kept coming back to the contention that it was he who should have gone before her. Insightfully, the psychologist helped him see that her predeceasing him did in fact serve a great purpose. It spared her the agony of being alone and heartbroken without him in her life. This realization was like a thunderbolt for the man and served as a balm for his broken heart. He found himself comforted by this new perspective, and the healing process was able to begin. At long last, he was able to move forward with his life.

Another case:

Rebecca, a troubled middle-aged woman, approached me to discuss a painful family situation. Her husband, Mark, was diagnosed with progressive kidney disease and was in desperate need of a kidney transplant. The doctors pointed out that if a family member would be a match, that would be the best bet. Her husband did, in fact, have a sister, Shirley, but most unfortunately they had been estranged from each other for years. Apparently, during a family feud that took place many years earlier, the two of them took opposite sides. Since then "the twain never met" and the chasm between them grew to become irreparable. Despite the passage of many years and many attempts at reconciliation, both siblings refused to budge from their intransigent positions. Currently, however, when learning of her brother's dire situation, Shirley emailed Rebecca, informing her that she had had herself tested and was found to be a perfect match for Mark. Moreover, she was eager and ready to do this for her brother. When Rebecca related this to Mark, his initial reaction was that under no circumstances would he allow his nemesis to save his life. Eventually, however, Shirley's persistent pleas softened his resistance, and a dialogue between them was initiated. They came to realize that the rift between them was one of having allowed separate realities to take root in their minds, poisoning their respective abilities to appreciate the possibility of variant conclusions. When, finally, they were able to listen to each other, to talk civilly and share their views, they ultimately were able to bridge the gap. Rebecca commented that it was so very sad that it took her husband's being on the edge, between life and death, to affect this change. However, with great gratitude and, as she put it, with G-d's help, not only would her husband's life be saved, but a long-lost relationship would be salvaged and reinstated.

Unquestionably, our personally generated perceptions create our realities. We tend to get so locked into one way of seeing things that all other roads appear to be dead ends. Invariably, we get trapped.

It is singularly tragic that the greatest damage inflicted by the inability to respect the thinking of others is in the realm of close relationships. When family members dig in their heels and insist on the verity of their own opinion, strife and heartache ensues, tearing loved ones apart.

If we examine the common denominator in the earlier noted anecdotes, we will find that they share the fatal flaw of seeing situations exclusively through the lenses and prisms of our own bias — our personal thinking and feelings. Listening and opening ourselves to more possibilities and perceptions can, at one and the same time, broaden our horizons and fill us with a sense of humility. Being inflexibly invested in our own thinking, on the other hand, keeps us confined in a very narrow space, obscuring much light and inviting impenetrable darkness.

It is important that, every now and again, we look at our lives and our relationships to identify the unnecessary barriers between ourselves and others. We need to make room for ways of thinking and views that are different than our own. Unquestionably, we will find that with objective scrutiny, on the broader landscape of life, these views might just turn out to be equally valid, and provide a bridge between ourselves and others that offers enrichment to all. Opening ourselves to other's views is the key to keeping relationships strong.

Esther, one of my clients, walked into my office in a state of terror. She related that her rabbi, in his Shabbos talk, had drawn an analogy between the four-fifths of Jews who perished in Egypt and the spiritual state of world Jewry in modern times. Most Jews in Egypt, he elaborated, were lost to assimilation, such that when the time came to go out only one-fifth qualified for the exodus to freedom.

Esther confided that the following night she had a horrific night-mare in which she was pleading with Moshiach to be allowed to join her brethren in the final redemption to Eretz Yisrael. It got her thinking. How many of us are spiritually ready for the ultimate redemption?

Indeed, Esther's nightmare should give all of us pause to reflect. Every morning we recite the *berachah* thanking Hashem "*shelo asani goy*," for not causing us to be born as non-Jews. The commentaries note that this is not a one-time declaration; that is, that we should not as-sume that once we are born Jewish we are therefore set for life. Rather, each morning upon awakening we need to revisit the question of how much of the non-Jewish world has inadvertently crept into our souls. We learn from the *berachah* that a Jew must constantly assess and reassess himself, taking a moral and spiritual inventory of his progress.

The paradigm of Moshe Rabbeinu is instructive in charting a course of spiritual survival while in *galus*. Our Sages teach that the first exile in *Mitzrayim* was the prototype for all subsequent exiles. They tell us that the first *galus* began when the eyes and hearts of the Jews were "plugged up." After the passing of our Patriarch Yaakov Avinu, the Jewish nation gradually lost its capacity to perceive the creeping descent into the abyss of Egyptian immorality. The seeds of redemption were planted when, as the verse reads, "the lad [Moshe] grew up and *saw*." Moshe Rabbeinu, a privileged child of the palace, left his comfort zone and went out to see the plight of his unfortunate brethren, who were subjected to a brutal and dehumanizing slavery. He chose to rise above indifference to the suffering of others.

Later, when shepherding his father-in-law's flock, he encountered the burning bush. "Let me turn aside [from my daily routine] and see this great sight, why the bush burns and is not consumed." Moshe Rabbeinu was drawn to a fire that wasn't subject to the laws of nature, a flame that refused to be extinguished. In our contemporary experience, that fire represents the presence of Hashem in our lives. No matter how dark or hopeless a situation may seem or how desperate we perceive ourselves to be, a fiery, infinite force exists that is available if we but choose to *see* it.

A relevant example of being aware of Hashem's presence occurred as I was penning these words. A young woman I had counseled on one of my out-of-town trips phoned to give me an update on her situation. Like so many others, unfortunately, her husband had lost his job and was unemployed for an extended period of time. In addition, several other challenges had arisen to create a truly dismal situation. At the time, I encouraged her to "go with the flow" and not allow the situation, grave as it was, to exact a price on her marriage. She was remarkably receptive, acknowledging that her husband was a fine person who definitely deserved her support. Her latest call was to let me know that, with Hashem's help, her husband had found a job. She was very grateful to the One Above. It struck me that she could have easily attributed this success to her husband's perseverance or his impressive résumé. Instead, she actively *saw* the loving hand of Hashem in her life.

Another example that comes to mind is my grandson Motty, whose kindergarten class was once offered a special treat. There was one boy, however, who suffered from terrible allergies and wasn't permitted to eat it. In a gesture of solidarity, Motty, sensitive to the plight of his classmate, also refused to accept it. I was touched and proud that such a young child understood the concept of "*imo anochi betzarah,*" of noticing and having empathy for another's suffering.

It also reminds me of an anecdote I once heard about a certain rabbi who got a phone call from someone he didn't know. After thanking the rabbi for taking his call, the man abruptly asked him to call back, ostensibly because he couldn't talk to him at that moment. Somewhat taken aback, the rabbi jotted down the phone number and resumed his busy schedule. A few days later he came across the slip of paper and dialed the number. Again, the man asked him to call him back. This scenario repeated itself three times. The rabbi was very puzzled. He didn't know this man, and it seemed very odd that a person would take the liberty of imposing himself so cavalierly on a stranger. Nonetheless, the rabbi called him again, at which point the man asked if they could meet in person.

It turned out that the man was a Holocaust survivor who had lost everything and everyone dear to him in life. His existence was so unbearably lonely that he had decided to put G-d to the test: He would make these strange phone calls to a rabbi he had chosen at random and see what happened. In his mind, a positive response would be a message from Hashem that despite his unfortunate circumstances, G-d still cared about him and wanted him in His world. The rabbi, in his act of noticing and mindfulness, had given another Jew the impetus to live.

The antidote to Esther's nightmare and for all of us in our dark, bitter *galus* (may it end very soon) is to counteract the blockage of our eyes and hearts by opening them wide and attentively. We need to see our fellow man and know that we are all in this together. We mustn't let our differences tear us apart. At the end of the day, we are all brothers and sisters — family — in the very deepest sense. We do not need the anti-Semitic world to remind us that the people of Israel are of one fabric, as it often has in the past.

Apropos is our Sages' explanation of the *Havdalah* prayer in which we bless "He Who distinguishes between the holy and the profane, between light and darkness, and between Israel and the nations." The distinction between "holy and profane" is our responsibility, and between "light and darkness" is the *Ribbono Shel Olam's* territory. The distinction between "Israel and the nations" is one that we, ourselves, should execute, but is sadly often usurped by the non-Jewish world, whose historical enmity reminds us that we are a people apart, most especially when *we* forget.

If every day we were to commit to an additional act of reaching out to another person and identifying Hashem's kindness in our lives, we would be following Moshe Rabbeinu's example. In so doing, we would unquestionably be part of Hashem's special legion poised for the final redemption, speedily in our day.

CHAPTER 6

Uniqueness

The practice in our shul is to sing "*Anim Zemiros*" at the conclusion of the Shabbos *Musaf* service. Typically, a young person leads the congregation in a responsive rendition, in the melody of his choice. Their young voices ringing out with the vitality of youth and innocence warm our hearts, and on a deeper level, infuse us with hope for the future.

On one recent *Yom Tov*, our grandson Shabse was home from yeshiva. Among his many other outstanding qualities is a beautiful singing voice. To my delight (and that of the entire shul), Shabse led us in the singing of the "*Anim Zemiros*." The tune he chose was the *niggun* that my father, *zt"l*, used for the *mitzvah tantz*. The memories triggered by this nostalgic melody transported me back many years. As I envisioned the band striking up the song, I saw my father's venerable, magical presence approaching us, his daughters, and in later years, his granddaughters, to engage us in that exalted "dance of mitzvah." Throughout his life, what set my father apart and made everything he did so memorable was that he invested everything he did with passion — with his heart and soul. There was nothing equivocal about him, whether addressing huge audiences with his magnificent oratorical skills or in his private interactions. It has been almost twenty-five years since his passing, yet those who encountered him still insist they feel his extraordinary impact.

At the beginning of *Parshas Beha'aloscha*, Rashi cites an interesting interaction between Hashem and Aharon HaKohen. Upon perceiving Aharon's dismay that neither he nor his tribe, the Levites, were accorded a role in the dedication of the *Mishkan* commensurate with that of the *Nesi'im* of the other tribes, Hashem reaches out to comfort him. "*Chayecha*," Hashem tells him. "Your role is greater than theirs, in that you and your descendants will have the mitzvah of preparing and lighting the Menorah."

The commentaries explain that the primacy of this function over the other rites rests in the fact that even after the destruction of the two *Batei Mikdash*, the lighting of the Chanukah Menorah would remain a vibrant part of the Jewish People's connection to the Holy Temple.

My husband, *shlita*, has noted that the word "*chayecha*," which opens Hashem's conversation with Aharon and is translated literally as "by your life," is an idiom generally taken to mean "I promise you." However, there is also an interpretation found in our holy *sefarim* that it is meant literally, in the sense that Hashem exclaimed, "Since your pain is so deep that it touches the very essence of your life, you have earned the privilege of lighting the Menorah in the *Mishkan* and Beis Hamikdash and even afterwards, when Israel will still have the Chanukah lights in your merit."

In other words, because Aharon invested so much of his passion and life force ("*chayecha*") in the desire for *avodas Hashem*, the lighting of the Menorah would have perpetuity, escorting him and his generations throughout history along with the rest of the Jewish nation.

Indeed, this leads us to a logical question: What generates a passionate response in our own lives? What excites us to the point that our "life" is virtually on the line? What do we consider to be so all-consuming and essential that it touches our very being?

- For some, it may (unfortunately) be business concerns that occupy front and center of their daily existence.

- Still others may be preoccupied with entertainment, recreation, and having fun.
- Others may be motivated by *ruchniyus*.
- The one thing that is incontrovertible is that a person's descendants will be impacted by whatever has the quality of *"chayecha"* as its momentum.

Consider Yitzchak, a successful businessman in our community who adopted a life of Torah and mitzvos later in life. This was a person determined to "catch up." Towards this end, he spent all of his spare time (and vacationed annually!) in Lakewood, under the tutelage of *yungeleit* he paid to learn Torah with him. On a regular basis, day in and day out, he woke up in the predawn hours to learn the sacred texts, and after work he followed up with more learning. Indeed, he became the living paradigm of our Sages's comment that "nothing stands in the way of one's will." Today, many years later, Yitzchak's family consists of *talmidei chachamim*, *ehrliche* sons and daughters who are unquestionably a result of his passionate dedication to Torah that drove and continues to drive his life.

A person's descendants will be impacted by whatever has the quality of "chayecha" as its momentum.

To me and my family, my siblings and their children, my father represented a trail blazed by *"chayecha"* — the investment of one's entire being for that which constitutes true "life" and makes it worthwhile, cogent, and coherent: *avodas Hashem* with fervor.

Indeed, the example of Aharon HaKohen and the Menorah's lights remind us that a wishy-washy approach to holiness is not what will ultimately usher in the redemption with Moshiach. Each of us has our own particular life experiences and purpose, yet only *"chayecha,"* living a purpose-driven life with zeal and passion, will get us to the long awaited finish line.

A disciple of my brother-in-law Rav Shlomo Twerski, *zt"l*, once asked him if he was trying to model himself after his father, Rav Yaakov Yisroel Twerski, *zt"l*. Rav Shlomo responded that that was indeed his intention. "My father was not an imitator or a copycat, and neither am I." In other words, he was copying him ... by not copying him.

> *My brother-in-law copied his father ... by*
> *not copying him.*

Implicit in his response was that Hashem created all of us as different and unique human beings, and that each of us must strive to become who *we* were meant to be. Our Sages note, "Just as people's faces are dissimilar from one another, so too is their essence different."

Consider Malky, who came in for her "annual spiritual." She is one of the many praiseworthy women who take introspection seriously. Malky reiterated her struggle of many years that she has as yet to resolve. Intellectually, she understands that the Master of the World "packs our suitcase," that it is He who determines the circumstances of our lives. Emotionally, however, Malky acknowledges that she can't come to terms with the fact that she didn't get the husband she idealized, the house of her dreams, financial security, etc. She confesses that she looks at the lives of those around her and envies what she perceives of as their charmed lives. Upon further inquiry, she admits that her spouse is a substantive person, extremely devoted to her and the family, a person who enjoys the respect of the community. Malky also concedes that her children are wonderful and that she wants for nothing. She has a roof over her head, food on the table, clothing to wear, the utilities paid — not luxuriance to be sure, but the basics. Objectively speaking, she lacks nothing.

In her mind, however, she lives an existence of deprivation. Malky would like to understand the "why" of the suitcase Hashem packed for her, including a childhood of abuse and an adulthood of protracted depression over her lot in life.

We discussed the fact that there is meaning and purpose to all challenges, and that along with the trials and tribulations, Hashem packed for us ample resources to cope with them. The caveat, however, is that we need to *choose* to use these resources effectively. Comparisons are irrelevant because other people's suitcases don't belong to us, and what each of us has to deal with is not arbitrary. Hashem, in His infinite wisdom, has a vision in mind of what each one of our contributions to the destiny of His world should be, and the tools for discharging our mission are the particular circumstances of our existence.

It is unquestionably a tall order. It is only human to want to be the one in charge; to be the one who writes the script and decides who gets what and when. I exhorted Malky to remember that an essential component of our faith in Divine Providence (*Hashgachah Pratis*) is the certitude that what we contend with comes from a G-d Who loves each and every one of us even more than a parent loves an only child. Hashem is not to be seen as a punitive being Who delights in our misery. He is on our team; indeed, He is *running* our team, and is rooting for us.

Our Sages comment that it is for this reason that G-d created Adam, the first human being on earth, as a "*yechidi,*" one person alone. Hashem, in His omnipotence, could have just as easily ordered, with a mere pronouncement, a universe immediately populated with billions of people. The creation of a single person, our Sages state, was a declaration to every person, past, present, and future, that in the eyes of the Creator, all of creation was worth it for his sake alone. Clearly, the message is how precious every "*neshamah*" is to Hashem. Moreover, it speaks to the fact that our mission is singular and specific to ourselves.

G-d created Adam as a "yechidi," one person alone.

He could have just as easily ordered,
with a mere pronouncement, a universe
immediately populated with billions of
people. But He didn't.

A parable that captures this message is told of a water carrier who daily delivered two pails of water to the king's palace. One of the two pails perched on his shoulder had a crack in it. By the time the water carrier arrived at the palace, half of the water in that pail had dripped out and was gone. Distressed, the pail complained to the carrier, pointing out how futile it was for him to schlep a damaged pail. "Why don't you just replace me," he cried, "with a fully functioning one?" In response, the water carrier directed the cracked pail to observe his side of the road on their next trip and report what he saw. As instructed, the pail noted beautiful flowers and vegetation on his side, whereas, surprisingly, the other side of the road was totally barren. "Don't you see," the water carrier explained, "the flaw in you was deliberate, so that you might water the seeds on your side of the road. What you thought to be a defect was, in reality, the specific mission assigned to you."

Reb Shlomo's insightful observation (that what he and his father had in common was that neither one of them was a copycat) speaks to the concept of celebrating distinctiveness, rather than resenting differences. It confirms the understanding that Hashem, in His great wisdom, assigned each of us equally important — albeit different — roles for us to use as we toil in "His vineyard."

To the extent that we can integrate this understanding, we will achieve a level of *"menuchas hanefesh,"* peace of mind, borne of energies liberated from the pointless quest of trying to be an "imitation" of someone else and envying "suitcases" that don't belong to us.

The subject of dreams, their definition, and their meanings have fascinated and captured the attention of many philosophers, psychiatrists, psychologists, and thinkers throughout the years.

The most basic definition of "dream," provided by the dictionary, is that of "something taught, felt, seen, or heard during sleep."

A second interpretation is "something unreal" as in one author's assessment of life, 'Life is an empty dream.'"

Indeed, this echoes Dovid Hamelech's exclamation of "When Hashem will return the captivity of Zion, we will be like dreamers" (*Tehillim* 126).

One of the renderings of this verse is that at the time of the ultimate redemption, the blinders will be removed from our eyes. Everything in our current existence, both the joys and vicissitudes that consume our every moment with an appearance of reality and urgency, will finally be seen as the illusion that they actually are. Just as one awakens from a dream that felt real when experienced, so too will we realize we were like "dreamers" in this "*olam hasheker*," in this world of illusion.

This understanding should perforce give us pause. It invites us to reflect on whether the things to which we dedicate our waking moments are worthy of so much attention and input. In fact, what will these look like to us, in retrospect, when the illusion is stripped away and we wake up from this life that is merely a "dream?

Yet another definition of dreams is that of "visions," fantasies, realizing a perfection only expected in a dream.

An instructive anecdote that captures this concept is one related about the Ponevezher Rav, *zt"l*, who is credited with the building of the city of Bnei Brak in Israel. At the time this story took place, Bnei Brak was a mere wilderness. The Ponevezher Rav was found by one of his disciples lost in thought, staring off into the distance, focusing on the view of the mountains on the horizon. The disciple asked the Ponevezher Rav, "What are you looking at, Rebbe? What do you see?" The Rebbe answered, "I see a bustling community. I see a yeshiva teeming with action, with hundreds of *talmidim* studying Torah." Taken aback, the student commented, "Rebbe, you are dreaming." "Yes," the Rebbe replied, "I am dreaming but I am not asleep." Indeed, today the thriving and flourishing Bnei Brak is a tribute to a man who dreamed, but because he was not asleep, he made it happen.

"I am dreaming but I am not asleep."

"Visions and fantasies" come to fruition and are realized only when one is not "asleep at the wheel," when one is willing to work hard and to expend the effort to make the dream become a reality.

A case in point is our Milwaukee community. Forty years ago, Milwaukee was no more than a spiritual wilderness. It was the "vision" of my husband, *shlita*, and like-minded supporters who mobilized to make the "impossible dream" happen. To say that there was no money would be an understatement, and, additionally, there was no support from the establishment. Quite the contrary, they and others in the community at large chose to place any possible impediments in our way. The journey was fraught with obstacle after obstacle. Unquestionably, the credit for our being able to successfully navigate this very challenging road was the "*siyata dishmaya*" (Heavenly assistance) that escorted us every step of the way. Moving forward, we pray that Hashem will continue to bless our efforts to sustain and maintain what was built. "*Siyata dishmaya*" notwithstanding, "*hishtadlus*," human input, is critical: hard work, determination, and the refusal to be disheartened or succumb to despair because of the many bumps along the road. Today, though still plagued by the occupational hazard of limited financial resources and the trials and tribulations of addressing the many complex human needs, *Baruch Hashem* we have shuls, schools at every level, and most significantly, a growth-oriented community dedicated to achieving ever greater heights in *avodas Hashem*.

I think it is fair to say that all of us entertain dreams. Many of us, however, dismiss them as mere fantasies that will never see the light of day. In great part, we feel that we are unworthy of achieving success in our endeavors. Who are we to have dreams? If "bigger" people haven't done "it," why should — or why can — we? We get bogged down by what we perceive of as the flaws and inadequacies in our person. We do a number on ourselves, beating ourselves up. Thus we are defeated — before we even begin.

An insightful and enlightening incident was recounted by an observer admiring the sculpture of a great artist. He asked the sculptor how he brought such beauty into being. After a moment's reflection, the sculptor replied, "When I look at a slab of marble, I have a vision of what it will look like, and I chip away whatever doesn't belong to that image."

Likewise, in the image and vision of what we might be, do, or accomplish, there will invariably be pieces that don't belong and possibly even get in our way of achieving our dream. Our task is to chip away and disabuse ourselves of that which blocks our path, be it external or internal.

Consider David, whose "dream" had always been to make a difference. His formative years were unremarkable. He was not among the strong learners. He recognized that scholarship and academic excellence were the currency of the society around him. Initially, he was disheartened, fearful that since he was not cut out to be a "*gadol hador*" or even a "*talmid chacham,*" there would be no respectful role for him to play. After much introspection, he concluded that achievement in the learning field was not the only avenue in which he could make a difference. He researched a business plan, worked hard to receive the necessary accreditations, and launched a very successful venture. He married, built a beautiful family, and currently supports countless Torah institutions. He prides himself in the fact that though he was a "failure" in his yeshiva days, he has not missed a day of being "*kovei'a itim,*" of designating time for learning. Aside from his own impressive learning, David says his main contribution is in the category of a "Zevulun," the tribe committed to supporting the "Yissachars," the learning tribe. To his credit, he understood that despite the efforts of the community in which he moved to marginalize the value of the "Zevuluns," his and theirs were on an equal par, of equal value.

Another example of the "ordinary" people in our midst who do the extraordinary and bring their dreams to life against great odds is Mildred. Mildred's parents divorced and left her life in shambles. She went through her teenage years adrift, trying to find her identity. Should she opt for the dissolute life of her mother or the "Jewishly" committed life of her father? Torn between loyalties and love for both of them, she ultimately reverted back to the "dream" of her youth lodged in her subconscious. She had always envisioned herself as the wife of a husband whom she could encourage to learn, as a mother of many children, and a leader in the field of education, providing opportunities for the disenfranchised. Resolute and determined, she did not allow doubts and the jaundiced views of her detractors to undermine her resolve. She moved forward to claim her dream. Today she is the head of a wonderful *Torah-dik* family.

There are dreams and there are dreams.

There are those whose substance is illusion, of living with impunity and disregarding what is real and enduring, and then there are dreams that are borne of the best and finest part of ourselves. Your dreams are not mine and mine are not yours. Our dreams reflect who we really are and what each of us is meant to achieve in this world. These dreams require "chipping away what doesn't belong," putting forth our best efforts, and with Hashem's help, turning these dreams into reality.

Among the many talents my husband denies having is the ability to compose music. He does compose melodies that are really quite inspiring, but he claims that these songs come *through* him rather than *from* him and so he can't take credit. Many of them are more traditional melodies that would probably not have wide appeal for a contemporary audience, but there is one group of people — those who are ill, depressed, or suffering in other ways — who seem to find a great deal of comfort in them.

Recently, I was about to leave the dentist's office when a woman I hardly recognized approached me and told me how delighted she was to see me. She related that her ninety-year-old mother, a Holocaust survivor who had suffered a stroke, had passed away recently in hospice care. No longer able to function or communicate, there was only one thing that had given her relief in her final days — my husband's music, which transported her to a happier place and time and soothed her profoundly. The woman continued that since her mother's passing, she herself has listened to it often. She asked me to let my husband know how very meaningful his music has been to both of them.

Although most of us do not have the gift of musical composition, we all play a vital role in the symphony of Hashem's world. Unfortunately, however, too many of us suffer from the feeling that we don't amount to much, that we don't have much to offer, and that we don't make a difference in the greater scheme of things. Our sense of worth is greatly lacking; hence, the proliferation of any number of books on self-esteem. From a Torah perspective, this void in self-regard is a very serious issue. The Kotzker Rebbe once commented that the greatest mistake — indeed, the greatest sin for a Jew — is to underestimate the self.

Rabbi Yaakov Solomon recently posted a story about Arturo Toscanini, one of the most acclaimed conductors of the late nineteenth and early twentieth centuries, who was renowned for his intensity, his restless perfectionism, his phenomenal ear for orchestral detail, and his photographic memory. Toscanini was sitting with his biographer one day, listening to a recording of a complicated overture. At the end, the maestro asked the author, "Did you notice anything unusual about what we just heard?"

"I have no idea," the writer confessed. "What was so unusual about this piece of music?"

"There should be fourteen violins. I heard only thirteen."

The biographer was astonished. How was it possible that Toscanini had discerned the absence of one violin? The next day he did some research and discovered that, in fact, one of the violinists had been absent when the recording was made.

Clearly, when an artist creates a work, he is deeply invested in making sure it meets exacting standards; there can be not even the smallest compromise.

Similarly, the *Ribbono Shel Olam* has created a magnificent, complex universe, a symphony of parts that work in harmony to produce the destiny that He envisions. The heavens, the sun, the stars, the fish, and the animals all sing *Perek Shirah*, paying tribute to Hashem for giving them roles in this glorious symphony. Human beings, Jews in particular, are the primary players, the *raison d'être* of creation. Each of us has his own unique piece to play, an individual contribution to make. Though at times we may think that the world would move along just fine without us, Hashem knows otherwise. Without our input, His symphony is incomplete.

Value can only be determined by the *Ribbono Shel Olam*. Some might argue that the only ones who matter are the prominent figures, the movers and shakers, but as is obvious in the world of music, the final product is the sum of every intricate detail — the loud and soft notes, the timing, the exact blend of instruments — with no one element more important than the others.

The Talmud (*Pesachim* 50a) tells of Rav Yosef the son of Rabbi Yehoshua ben Levi, who became so ill that his spirit left him. When he regained consciousness, his father asked him what he had seen in the World of Truth. Rav Yosef responded that he had seen an upside-down world; people who had been considered important when they were alive were diminished, while those who had led very quiet lives were highly regarded.

We must remember that the modest sounds in Hashem's symphony should not be underestimated. Hashem loves every single one of us — not on a comparative basis — and He greatly values our individual contributions.

My children gathered recently for a family *simchah* in Milwaukee. As I watched them interact, it struck me how the same set of parents can raise children who are so different from one another. Each one is unique, equally beloved and precious. Our perspective as parents enables us to understand the Divine perspective — that Hashem cherishes every single one of His children. Each one is priceless.

Hashem has created us, a family of people, and He celebrates our differences. We are the notes, the instruments, the rhythms — the sum and substance of harmony that will ultimately enable the world to complete its destiny. It is imperative that we overcome our sense of unworthiness, the belief that we are inconsequential.

Only when we learn to respect our roles in the universe will we feel up to facing the challenges life forces upon us. And when we take our places in the orchestra, when Hashem hears the glorious symphony of all of His children, we will certainly be blessed with the coming of Moshiach.

CHAPTER 7

Self-Confidence

M ark Twain once said, "I've suffered through so many things in my life, some of which actually happened."

His comment points us in the direction of recognizing that much of what we go through on a daily basis that affects our emotional wellbeing is generated by the hidden beliefs that we all have.

I've suffered through so many things in my life, some of which actually happened.

In a recent counseling session, Elana, a woman of exemplary character and a powerful activist in every worthy cause, shared her pain and frustration. She said that while she was able to tackle most things easily, there were some exceptions to the rule. What bothered her most was the way she handled her children upon their return from school. To her chagrin, Elana felt she was not as present, patient, and focused as she should be, and concluded that she must be a failure or an unfit mother. Elana did attribute her inability to cope to chronic sleep deprivation and a general state of exhaustion, but despite this, Elana's self-deprecation was palpable.

The counselor showed her that we all have an ideal picture of how we would want things to be. Elana ideally wanted to be more focused and present with her children. The practitioner further encouraged Elana to consider her subliminal, unexamined belief that when she was tired, her ability to "focus and be present" was grossly inadequate. In reality, however, there was no basis for that assumption, other than the hidden belief that was a product of her thinking. Elana realized that although she has less energy to cope with any given situation while tired, what she *can* offer is not without quality. If she assessed it objectively, she discovers that what she has left is more than adequate, her parenting is quite good, and she has every right to replace sinking feelings of inadequacy with feelings of competence.

When Elana realized that her response was created by her hidden beliefs, she felt liberated. She understood that her exhausted state did not necessarily impact her coping ability. Elana reported that, subsequently, when her children came home, instead of the familiar sinking feeling of a tired mother, she faced her hidden beliefs, dismissed them as an exaggeration, and embraced her children calmly and joyfully.

A similar scenario occurred with Jenny, a woman with a dynamic personality: bright, extroverted, funny, and delightful. Her two older sisters, powerful women who occupy prominent positions in their communities, were celebrated for public speaking, but being a public persona, especially public speaking, was not Jenny's "thing." While on vacation, the women in her hotel, familiar with her sisters' reputations as accomplished speakers, requested that Jenny address them that Shabbos. Jenny flatly refused; there was no way she would do this. Upon reflection, she realized that her resistance was a product of an unfounded conviction of ineptitude, only as real as she made it. Jenny then disregarded her inner misgivings and gave a resoundingly successful talk. More importantly, by recognizing the spell cast by her unchallenged conclusions, Jenny liberated herself from her hidden beliefs of inferiority and unleashed a new dimension of her potential.

> *Our thoughts ... are only thoughts.*

On a lighter note, I am working on my personal hidden belief — that I am hopelessly technologically challenged. My attempts to deal with cutting-edge devices, particularly the word processor upon which I draft my articles and publications, are disastrous. For a long time, I rationalized my perceived incompetence by claiming that contemporary media wastes precious time and can be spiritually compromising.

Once I understood that these conclusions came from subconscious feelings of technological insufficiency, I broke new ground in this area, despite doomsayers who insisted that I am a hopeless case. When I succeed, overcoming and mastering hitherto uncharted territory, I will, from a position of strength, declare them a waste of time. By then, the waters will not be muddied by mistaken assumptions, and what I will say will have more credibility.

> *We can indeed liberate ourselves from*
> *hidden feelings of inferiority.*

Confronting our hidden beliefs is not easy. They are longstanding and deeply rooted in our psyche. However, the recognition that our suppositions are no more than thoughts can render them powerless and make room for new thinking that can affirm and free the best parts of ourselves.

My husband and I recently experienced a heartrending situation. We were asked to participate in a consultation with the doctors of a young, beloved, terminally ill woman. The situation was bleak and the options were very limited. As one of the doctors put it, "We are between a rock and a hard place."

The scene was painful beyond words — tears, broken hearts, and excruciating life decisions. A young person on the brink of being whisked away, leaving a family behind — spouse, children, parents, siblings—all standing around helpless and grief-stricken.

In the midst of this grim picture, we were heartened to discover a sensitivity and level of concern from the medical personnel that comforted us. They were uncharacteristically and amazingly gentle and caring. They sat with us. They did not seem hurried or rushed. They explained. They answered questions with great solicitude. What struck us most, however, was their humility. They acknowledged and were aggrieved over the limitations of what medicine had to offer. With bowed heads, they deferred to a Higher Power.

Dr. Ari Kaz, an orthopedic surgeon and dear friend of the family, discussed a dilemma with which he had struggled before launching his practice. He said that in order for him to be a successful physician, he needed to be confident in the excellence of his skills, which he knew were considerable. Would that, he wondered, fly in the face of the humility that was so essential from a Torah perspective? He was advised by his rabbis that there was no contradiction between appreciating one's talents and being humble. The bridge that joined the two in perfect harmony was the understanding and acknowledgment that our competence in any given area is a gift from the Almighty; we are merely Hashem's instruments in this world.

A perfect case in point is Moshe Rabbeinu. The Torah attests that he was the most humble of all men. Yet, without a doubt, he knew that he was the scribe of the Torah — the person with whom Hashem had spoken, face-to-face. There was no denying his unique status and the role he played in the destiny of *Klal Yisrael*.

The caveat, however, was that Moshe Rabbeinu understood that G-d had chosen him. He was the Stradivarius, the violin, upon which Hashem played His music (*kaviyachol*). He was the vehicle (the *merkavah*), a magnificent one surely, to bring and manifest Hashem's message to the world. A total grasp of this reality was the sum and substance of Moshe Rabbeinu's humility.

The key to engaging life in a healthy, constructive, and productive way is not to disparage ourselves with thoughts of unworthiness. Quite the contrary, we need to acknowledge the many gifts and talents we possess. We need to give expression to them, be they manifestations of a brilliant mind, a kind heart, a helping hand, or a sympathetic ear. Wherever our individual abilities take us, our G-d-given mandate — our marching orders — are: "Go for it!"

The Zohar interprets the words in the Torah "to be fruitful and multiply" as referring not only to producing children, but also to producing the fruits of the talents with which Hashem has invested us.

In other words, the Torah is telling us to use our talents. Our gifts are not arbitrary or coincidental; Hashem gave them to us for the purpose of using them and enhancing His world.

The most common pitfall, however, is that we must be vigilant at all times not to take credit for our talents, not to attribute our individual gifts and successes to the ego, the self, but to maintain an awareness that, magnificent as we are, each of us is the handiwork of the Master of the world. We are His violin, designated each in our own way to play His music in His world.

> *We are Hashem's violin, designated each in our own way to play His music in His world.*

Someone once said that our deepest fear is not that we are inadequate — it is that we are incredibly powerful: It is our light, not our darkness, that most frightens us. We ask ourselves, "Who am I to be brilliant, gorgeous, talented, and fabulous?" Actually, who are you *not* to be? You are a child of G-d. Your playing small does not serve the world. There is nothing enlightened about shrinking so that other people won't feel insecure around you. You are meant to shine, as children do. We were born to make manifest the glory of Hashem that is within us. It's in each one of us. And as we let our own light shine, we unconsciously give other people permission to do the same.

At the end of the day, this is the definition of humility.

Over and over again, the Torah consistently points us in the direction of challenging the beliefs that constrain us.

A case in point is the narrative of the spies, who were sent to the Land of Israel to assess what the nation would encounter when they set out to conquer it. Regrettably, the scouts returned with a negative report. They related that giants inhabited the land and hence, "We were like grasshoppers in our eyes and so were we in their eyes."

It is difficult to understand this episode at face value. How could people who had just witnessed the astounding miracles Hashem performed on their behalf lose faith in His ability to help them? My husband, *shlita*, and others suggest that it wasn't faith in Hashem that was lacking; it was faith in themselves. In reality, "We were like grasshoppers in our own eyes," was their perception of themselves; it is only when one's sense of worth is diminished that "and so were we in their eyes" follows.

The way a person thinks about himself is projected outward. Indeed, it forms and shapes the opinion others will have of him. This is contrary to the typical, erroneous assumption that the opinion of others is responsible for our self-concept.

Clearly, life is created from the inside out. In truth, the way we think, carry, and comport ourselves determines the reality of our lives.

The Kotzker Rebbe concludes that the cardinal sin for a Jew is to underestimate himself, his inner resources, and his G-d-given abilities, which, if tapped, can propel a person to great heights.

After 210 years of servitude, the Jews in the desert had developed a slave mentality. They couldn't extricate themselves from the mistaken notion that their well-being and destiny lay in the hands of others. Indeed, it would take forty years of "reprogramming" for a new generation to emerge before they could enter the Promised Land.

All of us on a personal level have a "promised land," a place we dream about, a goal we would like to attain. Oftentimes, a shift in our thinking is all that is necessary to gain access to that place, which was previously out of bounds only because of self-limiting beliefs.

Consider the following examples:

- Sarah was a young woman who had been raised in a secular environment; she had never been exposed to anything Jewish. The first Shabbos she ever experienced was at our home when she was a college student. All I can say is that she was a sight to behold when she walked in — a beautiful blonde, immodestly attired and fitting all the stereotypes. I recently bumped into her when I presented at a women's conference. Still very beautiful but now dressed according to the dictates of *tzniyus*, she is a rebbetzin and a major force in outreach, teaching, counseling, and leading missions to Eretz Yisrael. Her sons and daughters are in yeshivos and *kollelim*. Sarah didn't allow thoughts of her limited background to imprison her. She believed in her ability to rise above her past and enter her "promised land."

- Mr. Richt was a Holocaust survivor who had lost his wife and child in the war. He related that on one occasion in the death camps, the Nazis made an announcement that they needed electricians. Mr. Richt, as witness to the daily carnage of the camps, watching his familiar landscape shrink quickly as loved ones, friends, and acquaintances disappeared one after the other, realized that it was inevitable that his number would come up soon. He decided that regardless of his total lack of experience, he would identify himself as an electrician. He was brought to an airplane factory and instructed to wire a plane in accordance with the electrical diagrams. He positioned himself next to a fellow who seemed to know what he was doing and took his cues from him; he basically faked it. Other people presented with a similar opportunity might have been intimidated by the challenge, but Mr. Richt's thoughts were solely to stay alive. In desperate perseverance he managed to outsmart the death machine. He survived the war, rebuilt his life, and served as the beloved *shamash* of our shul in Milwaukee for many years.

- David grew up in an abusive home. His father was a violent alcoholic who beat him, and his mother abandoned him at young age. His childhood was spent in a succession of foster homes and he ultimately ended up in an orphanage. But rather than view himself as a victim, he rose above his circumstances, became a professional of note, and raised a beautiful and spiritually-oriented family, serving as a role model for all who knew him. Again, he would have been entitled to a victim mentality. Instead, he chose to pick himself up out of the rubble and engage life meaningfully.

Each of these people — and each of us — could easily remain stuck with negative self-beliefs. The world provides enough of those. Still, when the circumstances and context of our lives don't provide a supportive cast, we dare not lose heart. From the "inside out," invoking the innate strength we all possess, we must always strive to be the instruments of our fate in order to gain entrance to our "promised land."

We can and must reevaluate our negative self-beliefs and always remember that we are talented, smart children of Hashem. The sky is the limit.

Our eight-year-old grandson, Shealeh, *yichyeh*, is reading a book on the Holocaust. The young lad is a thinker by nature, and exposure to that inferno and the unspeakable horrors visited upon our people has had a huge impact on him.

We recently had Shabbos dinner with our children, Shealeh's parents. Shealeh, whose anxieties were provoked by his reading, was very concerned about who was going to walk us home so that we arrive safely.

Young as he is, he has also been struck by the sheer heroism of the death camp prisoners and the ability of the human spirit to soar and triumph under the most horrific of circumstances. The accounts of *mesirus nefesh* and transcendence, of holding onto faith in Hashem and not betraying one's humanity are legion. On the one hand, they generate great pride in the caliber of the Jewish soul. On the other, they cause us to feel humble and wonder if, Heaven forbid, we were ever tested in a similar way, we would rise to the challenge. Would we be able to muster the requisite *emunah*, *bitachon*, and self-sacrifice to battle such an evil and formidable enemy?

An anecdote is told of a rebbe who asked his chassidim the following question: If they were walking down the street on Shabbos and saw a large sum of money on the ground, would they stoop to pick it up?

- One chassid insisted righteously that he would never desecrate the Shabbos.
- A second admitted with great sadness that given his state of poverty, he would likely fall victim to temptation.
- A third chassid came up with the answer the rebbe was looking for. He said that he knew what the ideal response *should* be and what he *should* do, yet he was also aware that theoretical predictions were useless and irrelevant. It is only when a person finds himself thrust into a given situation that his response will emerge, and one must hope and pray that he would prevail over evil.

We all have a tendency to underestimate ourselves. When we hear stories of those who preceded us, we convince ourselves that we could never measure up to their extraordinary achievements.

The truth, however, is that a definition of *mesirus nefesh*, self-sacrifice, is in order. We assume that surrendering one's life for Hashem constitutes the ultimate sacrifice. Arguably, however, the *sefarim* point out that living for Hashem in a transcendent way is a far greater accomplishment. Dying for Hashem takes but a moment; living an existence of *mesirus nefesh* is the path of a lifetime. *Mesirus nefesh* thus involves coming up against our perceived limitations and pushing out the walls of those boundaries. It means leaving our comfort zones and being willing to explore uncharted territory in personal growth.

> *We mistakenly think that surrendering one's*
> *life for Hashem is the ultimate achievement.*
> *But living for Hashem is a far greater*
> *accomplishment.*

Our Sages teach that the true greatness of Rachel Imeinu in transferring the codes to her sister Leah was not in her momentary flash of *mesirus nefesh*. Rather, it was the fact that in so doing she was willing to live the rest of her life, every single day, deprived of her intended husband, all for the sake of preventing her sister from being shamed and humiliated. Rachel did not know that her wicked father Lavan would allow Yaakov to work another seven years to earn her hand in marriage. *Mesirus nefesh* is thus the willingness to live day to day, moment to moment, with an awareness that every choice and decision we make is an opportunity for self-transcendence.

Consider for following stories:

- Dahlia was widowed, *r"l*, and left alone with a dozen children to raise. She was devastated and inconsolable. Nevertheless, she mobilized all of her strength to create a happy environment and a nurturing home for her children. Moreover, her acts of *chessed*, availing her many talents and gifts to whoever might benefit from them, were nothing short of remarkable.

- Henya's husband and family reeled from her negativity and dark moods. The shadows she cast over every situation were oppressive. She justified her attitude by claiming that her assessments were "realistic." When faced with a family member's life-threatening situation, Henya made a dramatic paradigm shift. After much laborious work and introspection, her gloomy and pessimistic stance gave way to a more upbeat disposition. To the delight of all she encountered, she began to exude a positive energy. She broke out of the habitual behavior that had imprisoned her for so long, transcending what she had insisted was just "her way" of thinking. *Mesirus nefesh* was invoked, and the greatest beneficiary of all was Henya herself.

- On a lighter note, my husband, *shlita*, claims great *mesirus nefesh* in that he has deferred to my preference for keeping the house at a cool temperature ("frigid," according to him) for the last fifty-plus years of our married life! [Since he has registered that complaint, I have attempted to stretch my tolerance for heat by hiking up the thermostat a few degrees.]

Someone aptly observed that great things in life are achieved not by extraordinary people but by ordinary people who do extraordinary things. That, in a nutshell, is the definition of *mesirus nefesh*.

Great things in life are achieved not by extraordinary people but by ordinary people who do extraordinary things.

Sarah walked into my office clearly distraught. She is an individual who takes life seriously, constantly striving, as she puts it, "to become a better person."

The source of her distress was that after occasional inspiration, the momentum for growth quickly faded away. Life as usual was taking over. She had "miles to go" of the formidable journey that awaited her, and she hadn't even taken the first step.

Sarah's dilemma is not an unfamiliar one. It is fair to say that at one time or another we have all suffered from this state of paralysis, caused by our perception that the goal is so distant from our present location that it doesn't even pay to try to move forward.

My son, Rav Efraim, *shlita*, of Chicago, shared a wonderful insight that sheds light on the impediments to growth we all face. He quoted the Zohar's interpretation of the first word of the Torah, "*bereishis*," as meaning "*beis reishis*," literally two beginnings or heads.

Usually, he explained, the work we have to do looms before us like a veritable ladder. We see ourselves as being at the very *bottom,* not having even ascended to the first rung. This perception is what drains our energy and demoralizes us. If instead of the bottom we saw ourselves as being at the *beginning,* our task would become much more doable. This approach would constitute the first of the two beginnings alluded to in the word *"bereishis."*

On a deeper level, this is the gist of the message Hashem gave Chava after she allowed the primordial serpent to persuade her to eat of the tree. We are taught that the snake represents the *yetzer hara,* the evil inclination. It is precisely the voice of this lesser part of ourselves that tries to convince us that we are at the bottom, and that the climb upward is far too steep for us to navigate. Hashem therefore tells Chava that "there will be enmity forever between you and the snake." This is the way the battle will shape up, Hashem told the snake: *"Hu yeshufcha rosh."* Man will be successful when he will trample you (the evil inclination) with *"rosh,"* when man views the road ahead as a beginning. You, the snake, will be victorious when *"teshufenu akeiv,"* when you will strike man with the pitfall of *"eikev,"* making him believe that he is at the bottom.

> *The Torah fully anticipates that our journey will include moments when we will seriously question our resolve.*

The Torah is realistic and fully anticipates that our journey will include moments when we will seriously question our resolve and good intentions. The voice of the snake that resides within us is ready and willing to undermine our every step. It will rear its ugly head time and again in its efforts to persuade us that we are at the bottom. Our response must be that, on the contrary, we are at the *"rosh,"* the beginning, however modest.

The second *"rosh"* of *"bereishis"* is when we reach our goal, the top of the ladder, only to realize that there are many more mountains to climb. We need to be clear about the fact that every step along the way is valuable and precious to the Master of the Universe.

The good news is that since our first session, Sarah has embraced the concept of beginnings and tried to implement it in her daily life. She reported that on a number of occasions recently she was able to resist sharing negative information with others. This was a departure from her previous habitual behavior and required a great deal of self-control on her part. It was a major victory for her, and although she understands that she might not always be successful, she felt empowered and good about herself. She had the sense that Hashem was at her side, proud and cheering her on. She had progressed from "bottoming out" to a solid "beginning." She was on her way!

We, too, can each be on our way. We're already there, actually. Pat yourself on the back — we are each at a new beginning. We've come so far, and Hashem will continue to help us achieve greatness.

CHAPTER 8

Moments

Time rushes by all too quickly. A case in point would be the long anticipated *Yom Tov* of Pesach, which seems to come and go in the blink of an eye. Even the many who tremble at the daunting task of preparing for and executing the many details of its celebration — the accommodations for visiting family, planning of menus, massive cleanup duties — surely concede that once Pesach made its appearance, they would have preferred it hadn't taken its leave so quickly, after a mere eight days.

As a member of the older generation, I find it fascinating to observe that the relationship to time is a product both of a given situation and one's stage in life. Consider how painfully slow time seems to pass when waiting for news of a loved one in surgery or a baby about to be born. Conversely, try as we might, we cannot seem to hang on to the time spent visiting with children or other joyous occasions. The conclusion we must arrive at is that the concept of time and how we interact with it is totally subjective; it is ours to define.

Consider Henny, a middle-aged woman who observed a hassled young mother scolding her little one in the checkout lane of a grocery store. Henny was overcome with a flashback of a similar incident with her now grown children. Unable to control her reminiscing, she turned to the young woman and said, "I know that this is unsolicited advice, but I strongly encourage you to enjoy these moments, because before you know it your children will be grown and out of the house."

I strongly encourage you to enjoy these moments.

I don't know if her counsel was welcomed, but I do know that I keep a picture on my refrigerator of my sons as youngsters hugging each other, and whenever I look at it I experience a tug in my heart. They were so cute and adorable, and I know for sure that I didn't appreciate them enough at the time. I was so busy (as are many young wives and mothers) with the many concerns for the future that the precious moments of the present were sometimes lost. I, like Henny, often wish to stop women who are so intent on the fast track and urge them to stop, breathe, and savor the moment.

Our *sefarim* teach that every moment in time is a world unto itself, never to appear again. It is distinct from the moment that precedes it and the one that follows. As such, each moment pleads with the human being to fill it with meaning, relish it, and give it perpetuity.

Let's consider together the following story:

The Rodishitzer Rebbe once visited an inn where he was assigned to a certain room. Later, the chassidim heard him dancing all night long. Knowing how exhausted the Rebbe had been from the journey, they couldn't contain their curiosity and questioned him in the morning.

In response, he summoned the proprietor and inquired about the origin of the clock in the room he had stayed in. The innkeeper explained that many years earlier the son of the Chozeh of Lublin had passed through, and in lieu of payment had given the innkeeper his revered father's clock.

This clock ticks to a different rhythm.

"That explains it!" the Rodishitzer exclaimed, and went on to relate that the clock on the wall of the room had ticked to a different rhythm than other clocks. The ticking of most clocks, he explained, is depressing, signaling the passage of time as if to say, "One moment gone, another moment gone ... "

This clock, however, had an upbeat tone, as if to proclaim, "One moment closer to Moshiach, another moment closer to Moshiach ..." Indeed, the sound of its ticking had inspired him to dance all night.

Time is fluid and marches on. Unquestionably, though, how we configure the ticking of our personal clock is up to us. Once again, it all comes down to our perspective.

The desire to run away from a difficult challenge is universal. Whether the context is marriage, employment, place of residence or a chosen course of study, when the going gets tough, many ordinary mortals flee the scene.

The following scenario is not at all uncommon:

Sarah tolerated an abusive and highly dysfunctional marriage for many years. Despite the pleas of family and friends, she elected to suffer humiliation and torment rather than seek a divorce. Finally, at the repeated urging of *rabbanim* and the intervention of therapists, she felt strong enough to stand up for herself and was successful in obtaining a *get*. Predictably, her initial reaction was euphoria. She was free at last. Also, predictably, the "high" that Sarah experienced did not last very long. While she had, at long last, achieved enough self-confidence and dignity to leave the marriage, she was ill-prepared to tackle what followed and get on with her life. Sarah's "high" gave way to a sinking feeling of "now what?"

There is a principle in physics asserting that nature abhors a vacuum. This same principle applies to our everyday pursuits and our emotional, intellectual, and spiritual activities. A new path or mode of behavior will inevitably replace the previous one to which we were accustomed.

> *Nature abhors a vacuum. True freedom*
> *requires a new path to replace the old one.*

The question then becomes, what exactly is going to take the place of the previous reality? The inescapable conclusion is that true freedom must consist of two phases: throwing off the shackles of our enslavement and having a plan for the future, i.e., freedom to do what?

This principle is also operative on the global stage. Witness the recent upheavals and revolutions in the Middle East and North Africa, known originally as the Arab Spring. Many governments were overthrown, but what has arisen in their place has not proven to be any better. The masses know what they *don't* want, but they have no cohesive plan as to what should follow the undoing of the previous system.

The Torah recognizes this phenomenon and addresses it in the connection between Pesach and Shavuos. Even before our liberation from slavery, Hashem outlined the objective of our soon-to-be-acquired freedom: "in order that you will serve Hashem on this mountain." While Pesach marked our liberation from the yoke of Pharaoh — phase one — Shavuos commemorates the giving of the Torah and our commitment to the yoke of mitzvos — phase two.

Since both phases are of one continuum, there are opinions that Pesach and Shavuos are really a single *Yom Tov*, and that the forty-nine days in between them are sort of a *"Chol Hamoed."* As such, it behooves us to examine the slave mentality and how we were able to sink to such a degraded state in Egypt. The Chasam Sofer offers a remarkable insight. The Egyptians, he explains, were able to demoralize *Klal Yisrael* and throw them into the abyss by convincing them that nothing they did mattered, and, by extension, that *they* didn't matter. They accomplished this by forcing the Jews to build structures that immediately crumbled and sank into the ground. All of the backbreaking labor to which the Jews were subjected was for naught. Indeed, when human beings toil day in and day out yet have nothing to show for their efforts, dehumanization ensues.

My father-in-law, *zt"l*, used to tell the story of a person who was falsely accused and sentenced to many years in prison. Before the guard locked the door to the cell, the man begged him for something useful to do while he was incarcerated. The guard took pity on the hapless fellow and pointed to a wheel protruding from the wall. Turning the wheel, he explained, would irrigate the surrounding fields and gardens, bringing life-giving waters to parched vegetation. Delighted, the prisoner spent years cranking the heavy wheel, imagining in his mind's-eye the flowers, grasses, and fruit trees he was causing to bloom and flourish. When the day of his release arrived, his first request was to see the results of his efforts. The guard broke into derisive laughter, revealing that the whole thing had been a hoax and that in fact the wheel was attached to absolutely nothing. The prisoner could not survive the knowledge that his labor had been in vain. He immediately collapsed and died.

After "phase one" of the liberation from slavery, Hashem declared us His chosen people and invested in us a piece of Himself, as it were. The Chasam Sofer interprets "I am Hashem, your G-d" (the first of the Ten Commandments) to mean "I am Hashem Who has given you *Elokecha*, a spark of G-dliness." This was "phase two," the knowledge that *everything* we do matters, because it comes from the G-dly self with which Hashem endows us.

The point is that if the Sarahs of the world — indeed, if any of us — are to be successful in their flight to freedom, they — we — must embark on a carefully devised program for the future. We need to find a constructive and productive path to replace the painful patterns of the past. True emancipation from our struggles requires connecting to our resilient core, doing some serious soul-searching, and looking inward. We can prevail and eschew doubts about our self-worth, for in truth, we are children of royalty. Every moment we live counts and has great value. Everything we do matters to our Heavenly Parent.

Victor Frankl, the Holocaust survivor and world-acclaimed psychiatrist, makes the following observation in his work *Man's Search for*

Meaning: "We have come to know man as he really is. After all, man is that being who invented the gas chambers of Auschwitz; however, he is also that being who entered those gas chambers upright with Hashem's prayer of *Shema Yisrael* on his lips."

I cited this quote at a speaking engagement on behalf of an organization called Kapayim. Kapayim provides assistance and comfort to families dealing with catastrophic illness, and is manned exclusively by volunteers who are nothing short of heroic in their unflagging support and encouragement. The event I was addressing paid tribute to the families who had demonstrated Herculean strength and courage in confronting their awesome challenges, and to the heartwarming help offered by the volunteers.

I subsequently heard through the grapevine that although, on the whole, the audience had found my remarks inspirational, a few women took exception to Victor Frankl's assignation of the term "man" to the Nazis, may their name be erased, who unleashed the most horrific evil upon our people.

Frankl recounts his heart-wrenching experiences in the camps with great poignancy. He describes not only the brutality of the SS guards, but with even greater pain, the cruelty of the kapos, the Jewish collaborators, which often exceeded that of their Nazi bosses.

The use of collaborators was not random. Analysts of the Nazi strategy to utilize Jews to oppress their own brethren have commented on the diabolic genius of the Germans in the dehumanization of their victims. They understood that appointing Jewish kapos would be the most potent psychological weapon to break the spirit of the Jewish prisoners and hasten their demise. As intolerable as it was to suffer unspeakable savagery at the hands of the Nazis, the complicity of the kapos caused agony that was beyond human endurance — their own 'brothers' dehumanized them as well!

It is hard to disagree with the objection of the women who felt that the appellations "man" and "Nazis" should not be uttered in the same sentence. Indeed, even calling them beasts would be an insult to animals. Animals kill only for utilitarian purposes, i.e., to satisfy their hunger. The Nazis murdered for no reason other than their virulent, satanic hatred of Jews.

While my inclusion of the two terms together was taken from an excerpt of Frankl's treatise, I apologized to those who found it offensive. Nevertheless, his point (that the human being has both the capacity to soar to the greatest heights, or, heaven forbid, to sink to the lowest depths of depravity) cannot be disputed, and his example is one of most effective we can use.

Human beings have both the capacity to soar to the greatest heights, or, heaven forbid, to sink to the lowest depths.

Let us examine the historical excellence of the Jewish nation in rising to unparalleled spiritual heights. Our holy *sefarim* define *mesirus nefesh* as the capacity to go beyond the limits of one's nature to the point of sacrificing one's life. As mentioned above, they expand this concept to mean not only dying *al kiddush Hashem*, but, even more significantly, living *al kiddush Hashem* — dying is a one-time sacrifice, but living for Hashem means transcending oneself constantly, a lifetime commitment to bringing *nachas* to our Creator in every expression and activity of life. Kapayim and many other magnificent organizations in the Jewish community, together with their inspired volunteers, are a testament to this phenomenon, and without question they constitute the highest order of *mesirus nefesh*. May Hashem bless all of them and those who support their efforts.

It is essential that we recognize that the Jewish People are not only blessed with a rich list of heroes from the distant past, but are equally fortunate to be able to look to contemporary heroes who personified a quintessential *mesirus nefesh*. Rabbi Meir Schuster, z"l, who passed away in 2014, comes to mind. I am proud to claim him as our own. It was in Milwaukee, with the Twerski family, that he found his path to Torah. He subsequently moved to Israel and established a wonderful family, with special kudos to his devoted wife who provided the support for his heroic *avodas hakodesh*. Reb Meir was singlehandedly responsible for returning thousands of people to Torah and mitzvos. Rav Noach Weinberg, *z"l*, of Aish HaTorah, referred to him as the paradigm of "the power of one." Reb Meir was a permanent fixture at the Kosel and the Egged bus station. His tall, lanky figure could be seen approaching the most unlikely candidates, inviting them to attend a Torah class or to join a *frum* family for a meal. Rejection was not an issue for him because his ego was non-existent. Reb Meir's sole objective was to bring Hashem's children back to their Heavenly Parent. He persisted with a genuineness that eventually won over even the most resistant of people. Reb Meir's *mesirus nefesh* was not only evident in his indefatigable determination to save Jewish *neshamos*, but in the nature of the personal effort itself.

Mesirus nefesh means not only dying
al kiddush Hashem, but, even more
significantly, living al kiddush Hashem.

This is so because objectively speaking, he would have been voted the least likely person to succeed at such an endeavor. Reb Meir, by nature, was painfully shy and perhaps even socially awkward. Unquestionably and admittedly, he was not a dynamic, charismatic figure. His sincerity, however, and his total lack of ulterior motives were the keys to his great achievements. He was truly a legend in our times and an inspiring example of the capacity for transcendence that marks the human being at his finest. May his memory be blessed.

Lest we entertain the illusion that the Kapayims and Reb Meir Schusters are rare exceptions in Jewish experience, let us remember that we are all the repository of potential greatness. If we choose to exercise our capacity for *mesirus nefesh* daily, in a myriad of ways, we can all be a source of light and inspiration to the world.

I am proud to say that much of what inspires me comes from the words and lessons of Torah I have heard from my husband, *shlita*, and wonderful sons, *sheyichyu*.

Occasionally, I find other sources of inspiration, including a particularly insightful remark made by one of my many precocious grandchildren. In fact, little Yossi's comment is worthy not only of chuckles but of serious reflection.

Many preschools and *chadarim* have a system whereby children bring in "mitzvah notes" attesting to their good behavior. Charming, devilish, and impish, Yossi pushes the limits at home, making the exercise of finding endorsements for his good behavior quite challenging. On this particular occasion, when his mother asked him what she should write he replied, "Write that *Ich folg der mama*" (I obey my mother). "When exactly did that happen?" she asked him accusingly. Without a moment's hesitation he responded, "*Fun heint un in vaiter vel ich folgen*" (From today onward I will behave).

Clearly nonplussed over his lapses in the past, he was poised to move on. Indeed, for him "today" was the first day of the rest of his life, and he had no intention of being defined or judged by what had already transpired.

My son, Reb Efraim, *shlita*, dwelled on this very concept in one of his *shiurim*. The Torah enjoins us to "be holy" in the present tense (*kedoshim tehiyu*). This would have seemed to be a tall order for a nation that was trying to make its way out of a spiritual morass that was unparalleled in history. How could a people who had sunk so low be exhorted to be holy?

The answer, he explained, relates to the ongoing battle of *Klal Yisrael* with its archenemy, Amalek. Our Sages teach that one of Moshe Rabbeinu's essential attributes was his approach of dealing with the "here and now." An example is found in the epic "*Az Yashir*," the song of thanksgiving, which Moshe led the nation in chanting at the miraculous event of the splitting of the sea. Moshe focused on the *moment*. He did not allow the anguish of the past or concerns for the future to derail him. Because this particular moment called for a triumphant song of gratitude, "*az yashir*," literally, "so then he sang."

This mode of interacting with life situations by capitalizing on the "now" serves as a lesson for our people.

Amalek, by contrast, is representative of all the detractors who attempt to undermine this most significant achievement. They try to do this by invoking "*machar*," the concept of *tomorrow*. The Amalekites of the world personify the demoralizing attitude that even if you happen to win the battle today, you will not be able to sustain that victory tomorrow. Why deceive yourself, Amalek scoffs, when you know that today's victory will be short-lived? Why even try?

Amalek scoffs: Don't you know
that today's victory will be short-lived?
Why even try?

Based on this insight, Moshe Rabbeinu's marching orders to Yehoshua take on new meaning: "Go out and wage war against Amalek tomorrow." The addition of the word "tomorrow" is not merely the "when" of the upcoming battle, but the definition of the enemy, whose stratagem is to sidetrack and deter us with the inevitable failures of tomorrow. As Jews, however, we know that it's the "now" that counts — regardless of the challenges the future may bring.

It is only human nature (especially after 210 years of slavery) that making a commitment to leading a disciplined life *forever* can be overwhelming and intimidating. Moshe Rabbeinu, in his G-d-inspired wisdom, knew that a person will respond affirmatively to doing Hashem's will *now* if we know that it will count and matter, even if one cannot promise with certitude that tomorrow will follow with equal success. In other words, the *now* is a great motivator because we can "handle" it.

Consider the fate of the many New Year's resolutions regarding diet and exercise. How long do they last? The thought of ongoing deprivation in the former case and of painful exertion in the latter, without the prospect of any letup, is too daunting a commitment for most. A more reasonable approach advocated by all therapeutic programs is to take on *one day* at a time.

My daughter Chagi told me that convincing her youngsters to give up their pacifiers for "just one day" worked wonders. Her earlier "forever" attempts invariably met with failure.

Another such case is Rachel, an acquaintance of mine, who thrived on sharing the latest news (bordering on gossip) with her friends. She was viewed as the clearing house for the latest in marriages, divorces, additions, and the acquisition of new homes. When Rachel was apprised of the serious violations that might be transgressed in disseminating such information indiscriminately, she was determined to "kick the habit." Rachel adopted a much more disciplined approach to the information she passed on. As she later related, her success in exercising self-control was due to dealing exclusively with the situation at hand, the now. She did not promise herself that she would never again engage in prohibited talk. That, Rachel believes, would have set her up for failure, but by framing the issue in the singular context of the immediate present, she was able to achieve mastery; the next moment would constitute its own challenge. In this way, Rachel progressively strengthened her spiritual muscles. In the exceptional instances of a lapse, she knew that her victories stood on their own merits and that nobody could take them away from her. This motivated her and kept her going, because at the end of the day she was able to see herself as a success rather than a failure.

We can all progressively strengthen our
spiritual muscles.

My grandson Yossi, young as he is, intuited correctly when he told his mother that although he hadn't lived up to the expectations of yesterday, there is a today and, with G-d's help, a tomorrow. Hope springs eternal where the future is concerned. Still, first and foremost we must invoke the policy of "*az*," making the current moment triumphant. We dare not lose out on the victories we can access — this very minute.

Elaine walked into my office, sat down, and began to sob. She proceeded to tell me about her beloved father, a prominent physician who had suffered a debilitating stroke. After six months of intensive re-habilitation, the doctors informed him and the family that the residual damage was irreversible, and that they couldn't see the possibility of his continuing the practice of medicine. From that point on, she related, her father had gone into a terrible depression. Medicine had been his whole life, and with that gone, he no longer wanted to live.

Scenarios of this kind are all too common in the world of secular en-deavor. When people put all their eggs in one basket and are exclusively focused on a single worldly pursuit, they run the risk of an irreconcilable void when that venture is no longer an option.

In one of his thought-provoking *shiurim*, my son, Rabbi Efraim, *shlita*, shared an interpretation of the Chasam Sofer on the *Birkas Kohanim*, the three-fold Priestly Blessing:

- The first segment, "May Hashem bless you and watch over you," refers to material beneficence and concludes with the word "*veyishmerecha*," the assurance that Hashem will watch over us so that His blessings will remains ours.
- The second part, "May Hashem shine His face upon you and give you favor," mitigates against others begrudging us our good fortune, thereby causing us harm. This is the implication of the word "*vichuneka*," which derives from the word "*chein*," meaning "favor." Hashem promises to draw positive feelings toward us so that everyone will rejoice in our good fortune.
- Finally, "May Hashem lift His face toward you and give you peace." Addressing the reality of human psychology, the Chasam Sofer notes our Sages' dictum that "he who has one portion wants two, and one who has a hundred desires two hundred, etc." The human frailty of greediness knows no bounds. The last part of the *Birkas Kohanim* is thus a blessing for peace of mind and a sense of contentment with what we have acquired.

And yet, as remarkable as these gifts are, the Chasam Sofer warns that they are insufficient, and draws our attention to the following verse in the Torah: "And they shall place My name upon the people of Israel and I will bless them."

Counterintuitive as it may seem, there is no greater challenge to a person than the unmitigated fruition of the Priestly Blessing. When all of these Divine promises are materialized and one finds himself gifted with all three facets: (1) material wealth protected by G-d; (2) favor in the eyes of others so that one's good fortune is secure; and (3) a sense of peace born of contentment with one's lot — one can too easily feel that there is nothing more for which to strive. His work is done. Confronted by a deep void, he seeks in vain to fill the emptiness. Frustration follows frustration until depression sets in.

Similarly, a lifetime of temporal accomplishments that comes to an end is a tragedy. This is the story of Elaine's father and many others like him, who, despite a lifetime of success, find themselves disoriented and tragically bereft of purpose.

The antidote to the "curse" of success is "And they shall place My name upon them and I will bless them." When a Jew invests in "My name" — in matters of spiritual growth and attainment — he always has something worthwhile for which to live. One never reaches the finish line. Even if one's physical world has collapsed, as long as the mind is intact there are always greater mountains to climb, more to learn, more heartfelt prayers to offer, and more opportunities to draw closer to Hashem. The life of the spirit is infinite. In the same way that the nature of physical strength is to wane with time, so is the nature of the spirit to expand with endless opportunities.

One never reaches the finish line.

Over the years, I have encountered many people whose investment in Torah and mitzvos was so essential that they lived for the day they could retire from the nitty-gritty concerns that consumed their time and energy and be free to devote themselves to the spiritual yearning that was the real force that drove their lives.

A case in point was my recent speaking engagement in Boca Raton, Florida, where a busload of people, most of whom were retirees, arrived from an area in the suburbs. One of the attendees shared with me that she and her husband had joined their retirement community precisely because it was comprised of people like them who were now able to pursue their dreams — attend classes, listen to *shiurim,* and pursue spiritual goals — something that was previously difficult given the obligations of making a living and raising a family. They were grateful for this deeper dimension in their golden years.

Whether this model or others, the quest for a relationship with the Master of the World never expires. While this particular group has the good fortune to maintain their vitality by turning to Torah, it is also true that one must exercise caution in postponing these aspirations for the distant future. Our *sifrei avodah* exhort us to cultivate an appreciation of the sublime even as we engage in the practical labors of our jobs and professions, or whatever else occupies the bulk of our time.

Both my mother and mother-in-law, z"l, when they were no longer the vibrant people they had been, remained connected with their Source, entering an other-worldly realm. The only words my mother uttered toward the end of her life were "thank you," "*baruch Hashem,*" and "Amen." My mother-in-law, with her memory virtually gone, expounded upon G-d's wondrous ways even to her non-Jewish caregivers.

The ability to live in a context of "placing My name upon them" requires a lifetime of immersion in the sacred — not necessarily time-wise (most people need to work, after all), but in terms of priority of values and an awareness of the presence of the *Ribbono Shel Olam* every step of the way. At the end of the day, what must permeate our consciousness is the understanding that He is the only reality that exists.

Elaine's father, unquestionably special and devoted, could not make the transition. When the life he knew was over, the proverbial rug was pulled out from under his feet. When people reminded him of his past great contributions to society in an attempt to comfort him, not only did it not help, but it reinforced his feeling that he was now a has-been, with nothing more to offer in his current state.

By contrast, those who are privileged to live in a Torah frame of reference will always find that when one door closes, another opens. It has been demonstrated that even in compromised states people can make invaluable contributions to their spiritual communities, even if it is no more than being a paragon of inspiration in how to deal with life when the chips are down.

When one door closes, another opens.

We have all come across individuals who bring equanimity, a steadfast will, and even a driving sense of purpose to their lives regardless of the circumstances that confront them. May we all find ourselves in the category of those who are able to "place Hashem's Name upon us" and never be subjected to the misfortune of perceiving our lives as irrelevant and with nowhere to go, and most importantly, bearers of Hashem's Name in all moments and every aspect of our lives.

Story #1

> *My husband was once summoned to the hospital where Sam, an elderly Holocaust survivor, was dying. Sam had never married, and his only relative was his sister, a spinster, who did not leave his bedside. My husband asked Sam if there was something he might bring him, anything that would cheer him up and give him pleasure.*
>
> *Sam thought for a moment and then said, "Rabbi, would you bring me a good piece of herring?"*
>
> *My husband assured him that he would feel privileged to do so.*
>
> *The life of a rabbi is demanding, with one moment and one task chasing the next. The days that ensued were particularly hectic, and a few days later we got a call informing*

us that Sam had passed away. When we paid a shivah call, Sam's sister informed us that the last thing he had said was, "Do you think the rabbi will still bring me that piece of herring?"

My husband was mortified and has since repeated this story many times. He would give anything to turn the clock back and redress his forgotten promise. Although he has sought forgiveness at Sam's graveside, his regret lingers on.

Story #2

David came to seek counsel about his ailing mother, who lived across the ocean. Paying her a visit would require a great deal of time away from work, and in addition, David would fall behind on the many other commitments in his life. Should he wait and see how she fared or should he go now? We advised him to go immediately. We had seen enough of life to know that the question one must ask under these circumstances is, "What will I regret the least in the future?" To the best of our knowledge, nobody has said that he wished he hadn't put himself out or gone the extra mile to see a parent or friend. Conversely, there are many who have expressed regret for not having seized the moment, difficult though it might have been, to be with a loved one at the right time.

There is a lesson here for all of us. We have opportunities on a daily, moment-to-moment basis to lift the spirits of a spouse, child, friend — anyone who crosses our path. As we have said, we can never adequately assess the impact or the ripple effect of a good word, a positive comment, or a loving embrace. No one ever knows what the next moment will bring. Hopefully, only good awaits us; but without a doubt, we will never have regrets if we leave a trail of kind and affirming gestures that gladden others' spirits.

Jewish celebrations present wonderful opportunities to meet interesting people who gather from near and far to share in the *simchah*. At a recent local bar mitzvah celebration, one of the out-of-town guests approached me to ask if she could speak to me privately. She gave the impression of being a very competent young woman, and we were able to find a few quiet moments to talk.

This woman, "Blimi," is an accomplished woman of considerable charm and the mother of several children. She told me about the life-threatening illness she had battled for several years, which, thank G-d, had ended well. The journey she described was quite amazing; she said she had surprised everyone, mostly herself, with the enormous strength and resilience she had summoned during months when she was wracked with unrelenting pain, maintaining her faith and equilibrium with great grace.

The paradox was that when she was finally able to return to normal life, she found that attending to her family's daily needs practically unraveled her. Amused and dismayed at the same time, she observed that while we can often muster the resources to ride out the big waves in life, the smaller ones can throw us off balance. It seems that the energy we often discover in a time of emergency isn't so readily available when it comes to our day-to-day challenges.

Blimi's experience is not an unfamiliar one.

We have all met people who have risen to great personal challenges with courage and poise. It behooves us to reflect on what gives us the fortitude and tenacity to ride the waves in certain circumstances, while in others we find ourselves sinking.

Because we are human, there are bound to be moments when we are less than perfect. At those times, faith wavers and frailty takes over. It is essential when that happens that we avoid judging ourselves too harshly. Spiritual clouds are part and parcel of the human condition; they move in to obscure the brightness of the sun, blocking our vision and causing us to lose perspective. Our negative thinking generates a state of confusion, and we thrash about, trying to regain our footing.

Spiritual clouds are part and parcel of the
human condition.

The good news is that, just as weather changes and clouds pass, our depressed thinking can shift and our vision can sharpen. We just have to be patient with ourselves and refrain from making any consequential decisions in those low moments. If we understand the simple truth that "this too shall pass," we can hang on, relax, and surrender to the wave.

A friend of mine, Karen, once spoke of the darkening effects of a necessary evening medication whose side effects included depression; it made her life seem worthless. What saved her was the knowledge that when the morning dawned, her mind would clear and her mood would be brighter. Understanding that her drug-induced state was temporary enabled her to tolerate those often frightening waves; she knew the shoreline would soon come into view. Karen's experience reminds us not to take our low moments too seriously.

A very wise, pious man once candidly acknowledged that he had seasons when he found himself losing his grip. At those times, he would open a siddur and daven, connecting to the only Truth that exists. A person's thoughts and feelings come and go, but Hashem — the Source of our ability to think and to feel — always was, is, and will be, in absolute perfection. This understanding can provide great comfort.

The Rambam advises that if we want to deepen our faith and grow to love and revere Hashem, we should observe nature, drinking in the majestic world that He has given us. Absorbing the beauty of our surroundings will restore our vision, reconnect us to the Divine, and help us recalibrate the thinking that drags us down.

The ability to ride the waves of our lives, both great and small, depends in great measure on our thinking. We have the unique ability to take command of our ship in even the most tempestuous waters and in life's difficult moments. But to do so, we must recognize the extent to which our thinking determines our reality. *Hashem Yisborach* has equipped us with the resources to transform challenges into opportunities for growth and advancement. With His help and the wise use of our *bechirah*, we can all ride the waves.

On a recent news program, a reporter expressed surprise that the public response to appeals for funds to combat the Ebola epidemic was disappointing. The contributions necessary to launch a major research initiative on this global menace were falling far short of expectations. Authorities were especially astounded since the Ebola virus was seen to constitute a very real peril to the entire world, and one would have expected an overwhelming response.

Mystified, they sought the input of psychologists who might help them understand the source of this widespread apathy. After considerable inquiry, the experts determined that people felt that no matter how much they did, the problem was so enormous that their personal contributions, no matter how generous, would not even make a dent in it. The enormity of the need and the hopelessness of the situation undermined the public's desire to help.

The psychologists suggested that people are looking for efficacy. They want to contribute to an effort or plan that will work. In the case of the Ebola outbreak, even if their money saved one person, they believed there would be thousands of others who would die. In contrast, donors responded more favorably to the hard-luck stories of individuals for whom their contribution might make a difference. The psychologists concluded that in order to engage people in any effort, a hopeful picture has to be presented.

Taking small, incremental steps is unquestionably the most effective approach when one is focused on growth. After all, *Chazal* warned: "*Tafasta merubah lo tafasta* — If you grab too much, you hold on to nothing."

The fact is that success, even in small increments, breeds success. When our modest efforts produce good results, faith in our ability is rekindled, and we are motivated to move forward. Conversely, if we seek to overhaul our lives in one fell swoop, the enormity of the undertaking will overwhelm us and defeat us before we begin.

The Midrash (*Parshas Nitzavim*) gives two examples of this principle. In the first, two men enter a shul full of people studying Torah. They are informed of the immense body of knowledge contained in the Torah. One of them, a *tipeish* (fool), quickly becomes overwhelmed, reasoning that since there is no way he will ever master so much material, he is better off not taking up the challenge. He throws up his hands in despair and walks out.

The second man, a *pikei'ach* (astute person), reasons that since all knowledge is acquired sentence by sentence, page by page, it behooves him — like every other scholar — to sit down and study, mastering whatever he can. Of course, the fool remains ignorant while the astute person thrives in his studies.

In another parable given by the Midrash, two individuals see a tantalizing pastry suspended from the ceiling. The *tipeish* says, "Who can reach that high?" and leaves, disappointed. The *pikei'ach* says, "If somebody was able to hang it that high, then there must be some way to get up there." He finds a ladder, retrieves the pastry, and enjoys his prize.

Consider the following contemporary scenarios:

- Suri bought into our culture's obsession with thinness, which has spawned many new diets over the past few decades. She said that when she recently looked in the mirror, she decided that this was the year she was going to return to her pre-marriage weight. Suri reported with considerable chagrin that after a few weeks, in her day-to-day struggle with a very restrictive diet, the image staring back at her in the mirror had been most uncharitable. Predictably, she began to feel like a total failure and was ready to abandon her resolve.
- Chani, a mother of six little ones, had resolved to daven *Shacharis* every morning. When her family and household duties simply did not allow for it, she became frustrated and disconcerted. To her credit, rather than abandoning her resolution, she decided

to modify her commitment, starting each day with the morning *berachos* and, if time allowed, adding one or two *tefillos* that she could invest with greater concentration. Chani recognized that every season in our lives requires different priorities, and that for a mother with small children, her *avodah* involved attending to their needs first.

• Gitty found herself in the "sandwich generation," caring for children, grandchildren, and elderly parents. Her plan for the coming year was to donate time and resources to some of the organizations that had reached out to her for help, but it became clear in short order that juggling her many responsibilities would not allow for the level of input she had envisioned. Gitty sought *daas Torah* and was told that her instinct to cut back on her communal activities was correct. She was told that she was spreading herself too thin and that everyone, herself included, would suffer in the process. She was advised to commit to one modest project that would not add undue stress to her life.

• Dassy was distressed because she had failed to carry out her commitment to control her stormy emotions. She had resolved on Rosh Hashanah never to get angry, to remain the picture of patience and calmness with her children, family, and friends. The very first time she lost her temper, despair set in. She termed herself a lost cause, someone who was irreversibly flawed. Dassy had managed to ignore the many times she had succeeded in controlling herself; she took her first failure to mean that she was a "loser."

The common denominator in these scenarios is the unrealistic nature of each person's resolution and her inability to take pride in small victories. Living a committed life involves growth, and growth, by definition, requires us to leave our comfort zone; but, as in all things, balance is necessary.

As the psychologists noted in their conclusions about the public response to the Ebola crisis, human beings are drawn to the doable. Undertaking a project that seems doomed from the outset drains our energy and makes it difficult for us to respect any strides we have made. In contrast, moving forward small step by small step, making modest, measurable progress (even succeeding for one moment!) is a much better guarantee that we will reach our G-d-given potential.

Human beings are drawn to the doable.

Our Sages teach that every moment of the day is an independent entity, separate from all those that came before it and all that will follow. As such, every moment pleads with us to invest it with purpose and meaning, as it is unique and will be in existence just this one time.

What, then, constitutes purpose and meaning? In the Hebrew language, *lashon hakodesh*, words and their roots are nuanced in such a way that they transmit voluminous insights. A case in point is the word "*netzach*," which means eternal and forever, sharing the same root as the word "*nitzachon*," meaning victory or triumph. The etymological intimation is that victory is only inherent in that which is eternal and forever. In considering how we should invest the precious moments of our lives, it behooves us to ask the question: "Is what I am about to do of a short-lived, transient nature, or am I making an acquisition in eternity?" Clearly, it is preferable to opt for that which is *netzach*, a segment of time captured forever.

Netzach, which means eternal, shares the same root as the word "nitzachon," meaning triumph.

Consider Chana, who grew up in a dysfunctional home. Her mother suffered from chronic depression and was seldom there for her. Her father was a bitter, frustrated person who lashed out in a verbally abusive manner. Chana's upbringing left much to be desired, with many lingering "scars" with which to contend. Chana, however, made a conscious decision that she would not allow her past to determine her future. She sought out and surrounded herself with positive and emotionally healthy people. She willfully and consciously created a happy environment for her husband and children. Chana viewed every moment as an opportunity to celebrate. Cooking, baking, and even cleaning filled her with joy. She thanked G-d for the privilege of being able to fulfill tasks and discharge responsibilities that others might have deemed menial and mundane. What many women considered pedestrian and burdensome chores, Chana saw as Divine gifts, all part of a seamless tapestry that would create positive memories for her family, something that she herself had never enjoyed. In so doing, she gave every moment eternal life.

It is essential to note that even moments that, strictly speaking, cannot be defined as "enjoyable" or "pleasant" can nonetheless be meaningful. An example of this would be Mindel, a middle-aged European woman who came to my attention recently. Mindel, I learned, had a young, newly-married daughter, Chavi, who had suffered a brain aneurysm, *r"l*, that put her into a coma for over a year. The family rallied around her in shifts around the clock. The hospital staff commented that they had never seen such an outpouring of love and devotion. Mindel, in particular, virtually never left her bedside. Throughout it all, despite the dire prognosis of the doctors, Mindel fully expected a miracle. She envisioned the great *kiddush Hashem* it would generate for both believers and nonbelievers alike.

Even moments that aren't "enjoyable" can
be meaningful.

Alas, such was not the intention of the Master of the World, and young Chavi succumbed to her illness. Though shattered and heartbroken, Mindel was determined that the *kiddush Hashem* would still take place. She continued visiting the hospital on a regular basis, providing comfort, encouragement, and solace to families dealing with similar challenges. Mindel became a virtual legend. Her broken heart became the catalyst for alleviating the pain and sorrow of others, and she dedicated her every act of *chessed* to the memory of her beloved daughter. Indeed, she captured all those moments for eternity, refusing to allow the scars of the past to determine her path in the future.

Whether with ecstatic joy or, *chas v'shalom*, in great pain, the *neshamah* of a Jew has the transformative power to convert an ephemeral moment to something so precious that the Creator deposits it into a vault of His greatest treasures. Rather than having to look back wistfully at time unwisely spent, let us seize the opportunity to invest our limited moments with a consciousness that preserves them forever with the *nitzachon* of *netzach*.

While in London on a recent trip for a grandchild's bris, we visited two of my husband's aunts, daughters of the Bobover Rebbe who was murdered by the Nazis. Now in their nineties, these aunts, both survivors, are the last vestiges of a bygone era in my husband's family. Their aristocratic origins are unmistakable; theirs is a beauty that years cannot erase. Sadly, their cognitive abilities are greatly diminished, and though they appeared thoroughly delighted to see us, it was questionable whether they knew who we were.

Nevertheless, they showered us with magnificent *berachos* and good wishes, a skill absorbed from many years of sitting at the feet of their illustrious father. I was reminded of the Bubbe Sura Maryum, an ancestress of these aunts and of my husband, who in her very old age was reputed to have told a visitor, "I don't know who I am. I also don't know where I am. But I do know *Whose* I am." There is no question that even when one's faculties are compromised, he or she still retains an essence, an awareness of what was primary in their lives.

> *"I don't know who I am. I also don't know where I am. But I do know Whose I am."*

In an effort to jog the memory of one of the aunts, we showed her a series of pictures, both old ones and more recent ones, of family members. None of them registered until we presented her with a picture of herself as a young girl some seventy years earlier. Instantly, there was a look of recognition, and she responded matter-of-factly, "That's me." What is so fascinating is that this was clearly the image she had of herself; in her mind's eye, she was still that beautiful young girl. I have met other elderly women who have shared similar perceptions of themselves; one friend in her late eighties told me that she still thought of herself as the tall, graceful creature of her youth.

We know that things are not as *they* are, but as *we* are. Each person's reality is subjective. I once heard someone remark, "It doesn't matter what his father was like; the only thing that matters is what *he* thinks his father was like." When we look out at the world, we don't see what is actually out there; we see an image of ourselves. The holy Baal Shem Tov taught that what we see in life is a reflection of who we are and what we are.

---

*Things are not as **they** are, but as **we** are.*

Other commentaries explain that the lens through which we see the world is a product of our cumulative wisdom. The reason we see things differently as we grow is because our wisdom has increased. We should bear in mind that there are endless levels of wisdom that can be accessed, and each time we climb to the next rung, our sense of reality perforce must change. Our understanding of reality is formed exclusively by the level of wisdom we have at any given moment.

The story is told of a mother who had twins with opposite dispositions; one was a bubbly optimist, the other a die-hard pessimist. Concerned about their extreme temperaments, she consulted a behavioral psychologist who was confident that he could "cure" them. He put the gloomy twin in a room with every conceivable toy and candy that a child could want and instructed the youngster to indulge himself freely, certain that the enchanting surroundings would cast a positive spell on him. He then placed the good-natured twin in a second room containing nothing but a pile of manure.

After some time had passed, confident that each twin's experience would have tempered his nature, he entered the first room, only to find the pessimistic twin sulking because the one toy he really wanted was not there. He then entered the second room. When he did not see the other twin, he called his name. The child peered out from the pile of manure and joyfully exclaimed, "I know there is a pony in here somewhere, and I am going to find it."

This story claims that a person's nature is immutable. It is a charming story — but is it true?

We have all encountered individuals who did not allow their natural inclination to dictate their perceptions. Consider Moishe, whose circumstances weighed heavily upon him. He was a member of the sandwich generation, trying desperately to care for his aging parents, his children, and his grandchildren. His burden was almost too great to bear, and he was noticeably dejected. But because he was a person of great integrity, he was disappointed in himself for not being able to summon genuine *simchas hachaim* despite his challenges. He struggled with this frustration and gradually realized that it was his thinking itself that was, in fact, prompting his depression.

He discovered that if he took a break in the middle of his difficult days and took a nap, he woke up in a very different mood. Sleep gave him a respite from his frenetic thinking, and when he awoke, his mind was calmer and he was able to come up with much better solutions to problems. Moishe found a way to change his thoughts and his life changed. He changed.

Similarly, an elderly woman in frail health was forced to move to a nursing home. When she arrived at her new residence, she was greeted by a social worker who escorted her to her room. In the elevator, the social worker launched into a colorful description of the woman's room. The new resident exclaimed, "Oh, I love it, I love it!"

"But you haven't seen it yet," the social worker responded.

"Let me tell you something, my dear," said the elderly woman. "Life is not about rearranging your furniture. It's about rearranging your thoughts."

Life is not about rearranging your furniture.
It's about rearranging your thoughts.

Whether we are optimists or pessimists, we all need to understand that it is not our circumstances that create our reality; rather, it is how we choose to interact with our circumstances that is the litmus test of who we truly are. Our perception of our challenges and opportunities, our surprises and disappointments, our successes and failures, is a barometer of the level of wisdom we have attained.

At any given moment, we might ask, "Mirror, mirror, on the wall, who am I, after all?"

When I walked out of the house to go to an eye doctor appointment, I was struck with a blast of bitter cold, biting air that all but knocked me over. Indeed, when I turned on the car radio they reported that with the wind chill, Milwaukee's current temperature was twenty-five degrees below zero. In an effort to make this frigid experience interesting for his frostbitten listeners, the meteorologist went on to say that scientists studying penguins who live in the Arctic Circle discovered that the penguins have lost their taste buds because they are subjected consistently to such bone-chilling, glacial cold.

I found myself chuckling at the prospect of practitioners in the weight-loss field applying this to those who are desperate to lose weight. Instead of recommending a few days at a spa, where certain painful diets are encouraged, many food types restricted, and more disciplined eating habits enforced, they might suggest a quick trip to the Arctic Circle where one's taste buds would be summarily destroyed, thereby rendering eating forbidden foods a non-issue. What a weight loss plan that would be! Needless to say, I don't think I'll be signing on anytime soon.

The above notwithstanding, there is a positive side to our inclement, snow-drenched climate, a dimension that impressed itself upon me as I was driving along on that wintry morning. Despite shivering body and chattering teeth, I could not help but behold the breathtakingly beautiful vista that filled the eye in all directions. It consisted of a pristine combination of a perfectly blue sky, an unbroken carpet of new, virgin snow, and a radiant sun reflected on the white mounds of snow in shimmering sparkles. My little grandson refers to these as "diamonds," strewn about by the Divine jeweler for our appreciation and enjoyment.

Additionally, as the scenery unfolded before me, a wave of nostalgia gripped my heart. I recalled that early in my marriage, my parents, z"l, used to schedule one of their annual visits to Milwaukee at this time of the year. Contrary to what one might think, my father loved this brutally cold season because the appearance of our neighborhood, with homes covered in a blanket of snow and icicles, along with the penetrating cold, reminded him of the "old country" and of his hometown, the shtetl in Europe from which he hailed. Every time we entered the warmth of our home from a brisk exposure to the outdoors, he would sit down and relate story after wonderful story, all ironically triggered by weather that most people would not cite as Milwaukee's most outstanding attraction.

My father's fascination with our winter climate prompted my recollection of an observation I once heard, that "one man's wilderness is another's theme park." In a less aesthetic way, this fact of life was further confirmed by an interview with the owner of a store that specialized in hot chocolate, who stated that the mind-numbing below-zero weather was actually wonderful for his business. Many frozen souls seeking respite from the severe outdoors were stopping in at the store to sit with a hot chocolate drink in front of a crackling fireplace. Since these were not conventional chocolate aficionados who ordinarily patronized his store, he welcomed the prosperity that, quite literally, the "wind blew in."

Indeed, "one man's wilderness is another's theme park." The phenomenon can even happen within the same person. Curses can indeed be blessings — and they often are.

I was taken aback when Debby, an attractive, successful, middle-aged social worker, shared that her recent life-threatening bout with cancer proved to be a positive turning point in her life. As strange as it may sound, she benefited greatly from her diagnosis. Debby explained that up to that point she had been working three jobs and felt compelled to take on whatever came her way. The diagnosis, in her words, gave her "permission" to slow down, to catch her breath, and live life more reasonably. She now has time to enjoy family and friends in a way that prior to her diagnosis she would have considered a luxury she could not afford to indulge in.

The issue of maturing (not of aging, Heaven forbid!) unquestionably brings in its wake a diminution in what heretofore one has taken for granted. The ability to see as sharply as in one's youth is often decreased, the capacity to hear as clearly as in the past is compromised, etc. But, again, there can be a "silver lining" in every storm cloud. Lisa claims that her waning eyesight and the dim lighting in her bedroom effectively serve to keep the wrinkles on her face mercifully, if not completely, out of sight — or at least less pronounced. As such, the times she has to confront the reality of her situation are reduced in frequency. "A blessing in disguise," is what she refers to that which others might view quite differently.

My mother-in-law, a woman of great substance, used to say that, without a doubt, the severe hearing loss she suffered with age was not always pleasant. The need to ask others to repeat their remarks, and the feeling of not being able to participate in group conversations certainly left something to be desired. On the other hand, she claimed that she was grateful that her condition spared her the need to listen to idle chatter and talk that was not of interest to her, and certainly not of the most exalted variety.

My father used to explain that the morning *tefillah* (prayer) thanking Hashem for being "*mechadesh*," of renewing the acts of creation daily, speaks to this very concept. First, we acknowledge that, on an ongoing basis, Hashem infuses creation with the energy for continued existence. At another level, my father stated, Hashem has also invested the human being with the ability to see creation and everything therein with a "new set of eyes" on a daily basis. We are not locked into a single way of thinking or of perceiving our reality. The "*chiddush*," the renewal, the ability to interpret our world from a fresh and more productive perspective, is in our hands.

Circumstances and situations in life are never objective. They are always subjective. Whether it is different people or the same person at different times, whether it is different situations or the same situation at different times, what we observe can either appear as a "wilderness" or a "theme park." Knowing that nothing is written in stone, and that moment to moment our perspective may change, enables us to hold a brush to the canvas of our lives, changing colors, contours, and landscapes in ever more intriguing and exciting variations. In truth, Hashem has invested us with the power to make life a beautiful adventure. And we thank Him with boundless gratitude for that!

My father-in-law, Rabbi Yaakov Yisroel Twerski, *zt"l*, passed away more than forty years ago, but despite the passage of time, the lessons he taught us remain fresh and inspiring. He was truly an extraordinary human being. In contrast to dignitaries who revel in public appearances, my father-in-law shunned the limelight. He seldom gave lectures or speeches; his genius lay in his ability to relate to people on a personal level. Everyone insisted that the "Rebbe" was his best friend. His daily activities consisted of visiting hospitals, comforting wounded hearts, and being there for everyone regardless of affiliation, both in times of need and of joy. A famous woman once observed that it is not what you say or do, but how you make a person feel that matters. My father-in-law had the uncanny ability to uplift everyone who crossed his path. He was beloved and revered in every precinct.

One of his pet peeves was that doctors had adopted the practice of apprising patients of their conditions, holding back nothing. My father-in-law was terribly distressed by this philosophy of "full disclosure." He maintained that giving patients a pessimistic prognosis — even if it was "accurate" in medical terms — was a virtual death sentence that robbed them of the desire to persevere and put up a fight. In his opinion, doctors were consigning patients to an inescapable fate and denying them hope, which is critical to a patient's well-being. He bemoaned the "G-d complex" of the medical establishment. Who are doctors, he questioned, to pronounce a situation hopeless?

What is interesting to me is that the current literature is very supportive of my father-in-law's argument. The mind-body connection is increasingly recognized as a major factor in healing and well-being. In a recent book entitled *Kidding Ourselves: The Hidden Power of Self-Deception*, former *Wall Street Journal* reporter Joseph T. Hallinan posits that perceiving ourselves as better, smarter, and more powerful than we actually are can set us up for greater health, happiness, and success. "When I started researching self-delusion," he writes, "I had no idea that it could translate into real benefits." One of these, he asserts, is that it gives one the illusion of control. Research suggests that control is essential to well-being. When a person feels powerless, stress hormones flood the system and wear out the body over time. One study found that workers who had little say over their schedules died earlier than people who could decide when to eat their lunch.

A sense of control is essential to well-being.

Interestingly, he notes several ways in which the world conspires to give us the perception of control. Take crosswalk buttons, for example. In New York City, most of them were disabled when traffic lights became computerized so they produced only a placebo effect; the "Walk" sign eventually appeared so people believed they had a hand in making it happen.

The same thing is said of office thermostats. By some estimates, the percentage of fake thermostats in office buildings is as high as ninety percent! They were installed solely to give employees the illusion of control over their environments.

Self-deception, Mr. Hallinan claims, is also a factor in a person's work performance. The worker who is fooling himself with an optimistic view of his abilities actually outranks his more realistic counterpart. Why? The more optimistic one is, the more likely he is to seize opportunities and take risks.

He warns, however, that there is also a downside. Self-deception to an extreme can cause a person to feel invincible and "drunk with power," and thereby lead him to destructive behaviors.

The author's conclusion is that believing in something, even though it cannot be empirically proven, gives one a greater edge to actually make things happen.

For us Jews, this concept is rooted in our being a supernatural people. At the inception of our nationhood, Hashem lifted Avraham, our first Patriarch, above the stars and instructed him to look down from that transcendent vantage point. Our Sages comment that by doing so, the Master of the Universe was informing Avraham that he and his descendants would have the ability to rise above the stars and defy the astrological influences that govern and limit the rest of humanity. Countless powerful nations have come and gone; yet tiny Israel, one sheep amongst many wolves, survives and enriches the world with its spiritual and intellectual vitality. With the help of the Almighty, Who has placed us above the stars, we have persevered and prospered, frustrating the predictions of our detractors.

On a personal level, we, like all others, seek the illusion of control in our daily lives, moment to moment. The Torah respects this basic human need and directs us to the areas in which we can and should exercise control.

When Moshe Rabbeinu questions whether the Jewish People will believe that he has been commissioned by Hashem to redeem them, Hashem asks him, "*Mah zeh beyadcha*" — what do you have in your hand? Moshe replies that he has a "*mateh*," a staff. One of the commentaries notes that the deeper meaning of this exchange was that Hashem was asking Moshe Rabbeinu to consider the parameters of his power and control. Moshe's insightful response was that the only thing "in his hand," the exclusive area of his control, was to be *"mateh,"* from the root word *"lehatos,"* meaning to turn in a given direction, a reference to *bechirah*, the ability to choose between good and evil. Additionally, a staff allows a person to point at the item of his choice. Hence, the message to Moshe was that the only control given to man is in choosing the direction in which he wishes to go.

> *In truth, the only control given to man is in choosing the direction in which he wishes to go.*

The ability to control our environment is wishful thinking and derives from self-deception. The only genuine choices and decisions we can make are in the spiritual realm; that is, when "the staff is in our hands." When it comes to matters of character and *ruchniyus*, *Bnei Yisrael* tower above the stars and control their destiny.

Pronouncements and predictions of doom and gloom by doctors and scientists, or even those of a positive variety, need to be taken with a grain of salt. At the end of the day, we believers, the children of believers, know that G-d runs the world and, as such, the possibilities of our lives — and of each and every one of our moments — are infinite.

Someone once aptly observed that when we are young we learn, and when we age we understand.

We often go about our daily lives under the illusion that human beings are capable of being in complete control. We move about the world thinking that the manipulation of our circumstances will bring us the desired results. While there is no question that we are called upon to put forth our best efforts to juggle the particulars of our existence and use our limited moments on this earth to their fullest, it behooves us to recognize that, in essence, success is determined by the Almighty alone.

Consider the following:

- An aviation expert was once invited to elaborate on the latest advances in the construction of aircraft. In his presentation, he noted that while the industry has come a long way in terms of newer and updated models, one cannot escape the fact that despite the most cutting-edge technology, airborne vehicles will always be at the mercy of the winds. Clearly what he was saying is that man's input can go just so far, but that G-d, Master of the winds, is still in absolute charge.

- Some years back my friend Harriet, a resident of Miami Beach, boasted that because she is such a super-organized *balebusta*, here she was, weeks before her son's upcoming bar mitzvah, and all the food was cooked and stored in the freezer. Lo and behold, to the horror of all Floridians, one of the worst hurricanes in history hit the coast just days before the event. The power was out for days; in some areas it was weeks before the electricity came on again. All of the food in Harriet's freezer was spoiled. The *simchah* had to be postponed for a later, gentler time. Once again, it was a painful reminder that "the best laid plans of mice and men often go astray," or as we say in Yiddish, "*a mentsch tracht un G-t lacht*" (man plans and G-d laughs).

- The day of Henchie's youngest daughter's wedding had finally arrived, dawning with a glorious June sun and perfectly blue sky. Henchie breathed a sigh of relief. Everyone was outfitted for the wedding and the many hitches she had feared had fortunately not come to pass. As they marched down to the *chuppah*, Henchie felt her face rapidly swelling up. Within minutes she was swept away to the nearest emergency room for evaluation; it turned out to be a severe allergic reaction. She missed the entire wedding. The good news, however, as Henchie reminds everyone, is that her couple is ecstatically happy, and "it will certainly go down in our family's history as a most memorable event."

These experiences serve to further verify that while we are obligated to invest reasonable *hishtadlus* to navigate our days, we dare not lose sight of the fact that it is ultimately Hashem Who controls all events. It is He who calls all the shots, and if we think we have control, we are buying into the supreme illusion.

In one of his recent *divrei Torah*, my husband referred to our Sages' statement that there are three "keys" that are exclusively within Hashem's domain: the key to birth; the key to rain; and the key to "*techiyas hameisim*," the resurrection of the dead.

In recent times, science has tried to arrive at complete mastery over the phenomenon of birth, and while inroads have certainly been made in facilitating pregnancies and the birthing process, the actual miracle of the creation of life remains within the purview of the Almighty.

The same is true with regard to rain. The ability to either bring it about or prevent it has consistently eluded the scientific community.

Of course, resurrection of the dead is an area that is still in the realm of science fiction (although the researchers are working on it!).

These three areas are representative of all aspects of life over which we would wish to assume control but sooner or later meet with futility. However, while the keys to birth, rain, and resurrection in the literal sense are not in our hands, a broader interpretation *does* allow for human intervention. Created in the image of our Maker, we too rule over these spheres in our own personal universe:

- The ability to give birth to a new spiritual initiative, opening a fresh chapter in the development of our *neshamah*, is a key that we actually do possess.
- Watering, nurturing and sustaining the newborn seed parallels the phenomenon of rain, which is yet another key we control.
- Finally, resurrection refers to the times in our lives when, having embarked on a positive path, we somehow stumble and fall, succumbing to pitfalls along the way. Yet, we must not despair or lose heart. The key to resurrection is in our hands if we elect to use it. Granted, overcoming failure demands determination and courage, but the wherewithal to start over again is something we can always access.

Thus when it comes to the physical circumstances of a person's life, i.e., birth, rain, and resurrection, G-d is in control. However, in matters of the soul, Hashem has given man *bechirah*, free will and the ability to make choices. In this sense, we are the ones who call the shots. Of course, even in matters of the spirit we need to call upon Hashem's assistance.

> *When it comes to the physical circumstances of a person's life, i.e., birth, rain, and resurrection, G-d is in control. However, in matters of the soul, He has given man bechirah, free will and the ability to make choices.*

May Hashem bless us with an understanding "borne of age." The courage to change the things that we can change; the serenity to accept the things that we cannot; and the wisdom to know the difference.

One of the perks of growing older is a role reversal in which parents find themselves the object of concern to their children, who worry excessively about their elders' physical well-being. In our case, one expression of this anxiety is our children's annual insistence that we escape the frigid Milwaukee winter for a milder clime, where there is less likelihood of slipping on icy sidewalks and hurting ourselves.

In truth, there is something to be said for blue skies, bright sunshine, and gentle breezes. Traveling to and from these earthly paradises, however, is quite another thing. Airport check-ins, long security lines, even longer treks to distant departure gates, and sitting many hours confined to narrow seats is no picnic for senior citizens. Most challenging of all is contending with planes that don't take off when they're supposed to, cancelled flights, and weather systems that rarely cooperate with one's plans.

A couple of years ago, my husband, *shlita*, and I were finally on our way back home from our winter exile. Our itinerary called for us to return to Milwaukee via Dallas, with ample time between connecting flights. Much to our delight, the plane that was to take us to Dallas arrived in a timely fashion, and we watched the inbound passengers deplane, eagerly anticipating that we would soon be on our way. We were about to board when the gate personnel announced a short delay due to the fact that they couldn't get the cargo doors open; hence, baggage couldn't be loaded or unloaded.

Fifteen minutes, an hour, two hours, three hours passed and still no luck. I told my daughter, who was checking in regularly on the old folks' progress, that she should consider dispatching our grandchildren to the scene. Without a doubt, they would have figured out how to get those doors open in a jiffy. The cynic in me was pondering how we could get a man to the moon but couldn't open a cargo door on a routine domestic flight!

When it ultimately became clear that we weren't going to make our connection in Dallas, we frantically sought an alternative way to get home. We were fortunately able to book a flight to Chicago that had been cancelled earlier because of an unexplained water leak and was rescheduled to leave eight hours later. With Hashem's help, we would be landing in Chicago at 1:30 a.m. and then face another two hours of travel time on the ground to Milwaukee. In my state of utter exhaustion, the cynic in me again piped up that I could have at least enjoyed another cup of coffee with my daughter, son-in-law, and grandchildren!

In an attempt to find a silver lining in this cloud, my husband gleaned a Torah thought that he shared with the shul community the following Shabbos. In Judaism, he explained, the journey trumps the destination. The journey is made up of our *hishtadlus*, our step-by-step efforts to live each day — and each moment — according to Hashem's will, being faithful to His precepts. By contrast, the destination, and whether or not we arrive there, is Hashem's department. My husband pointed to the *tefillah* that is said at the conclusion of learning a tractate of the Talmud: "They toil and we toil; we toil and are rewarded, while they [the nations of the world] toil and are not rewarded."

This statement is puzzling, because the nations of the world are frequently compensated for their hard work, and just as often, Jews aren't!

However, what is meant is that even when we don't produce, even when we aren't "successful" and don't achieve our "goals," we still receive reward. This is because it is the journey that ultimately counts. In the final analysis, every step along the way is what is precious in Hashem's eyes and what He seeks to recognize.

This insight is captured in the Torah's description of Amalek, the arch-enemy of Israel whom we are commanded to hate and destroy. The verse describes Amalek's detestable and unprovoked attack on *Bnei Yisrael* as "*asher karcha baderech*," they happened upon you along the way. Many commentaries draw our attention to another meaning of the word "*karcha*" (cooled you off).

This can be understood as "beware of Amalek who cooled you off" to the vital role of "*derech*," the importance of the journey that is so integral to Jewish life. Amalek focuses on results. In worldly matters, one can spend a lifetime pursuing a goal, a business venture, a literary achievement, or medical discovery, and in the event the goal is not reached, all is lost. The hapless individual is then defined as a "failure."

> Beware of Amalek who "cooled you off" to
> the vital role of "derech" — the vital role of
> the journey itself.

Our gratitude, as articulated in the aforementioned *tefillah*, is for the blessing of never having to confront this futility.

Given this insight, our trip home took on new meaning. In retrospect, were we grumbling and indignant or in a pleasant mood? Did we use our time productively or wastefully? Did we see the Hand of *hashgachah pratis* or attribute everything to happenstance and "bad luck?"

We certainly learned something about the definition of friendship from devoted friends who ventured out to Chicago in the wee hours of the morning to pick us up and didn't return home until 4:00 a.m. We were also most grateful for our own beds, as well as our children, grandchildren, and community. We were home, at long last, the lengthy journey notwithstanding. But it was precisely our long and complicated journey that made our homecoming all the more special.

A widely known quote from the ancient Kabbalistic *Sefer Yetzirah,* the Book of Creation, describes three fundamental properties of creation: *olam* (space), *shanah* (time), and *nefesh* (life).

The sacred texts comment that not only do these qualities define all existence, but also that the *Ribbono Shel Olam* uses them to communicate with us. Thus, the universe speaks to us, as does the calendar, and as does life itself. The crucial question is: How often do we listen?

It is told that the Toldos Yaakov Yosef, rabbi of Pulna'ah, a foremost disciple of the Baal Shem Tov (and perhaps his greatest scribe), was not originally of the chassidic persuasion. Indeed, he was at first bitterly opposed to the Baal Shem Tov and his teachings. The chassidic master, however, discerned the young rabbi's potential and sought to enlist the Toldos's great genius in the nascent movement's progress. During one early encounter with the Toldos, the Baal Shem vigorously argued the universality of the above principle and insisted that the rabbi of Pulna'ah was guilty of not listening to the messages that Hashem was sending him in many subtle ways. The Toldos heatedly contested this assertion and countered that ordinary folk were unworthy of such Divine messages.

In the middle of the discussion, there was a knock on the door and Ivan, a non-Jewish handyman, inquired if there was anything to fix around the house. The *Rebbe* referred the question to the Rebbetzin and reported back to Ivan that there was nothing that required repair. Disappointed, Ivan shouted, "That's impossible; there is always something to repair."

The Baal Shem Tov turned to the Toldos and said, "Did you hear that? He said there is always something to mend. Don't you see that as a message sent to us from Heaven? Isn't that true of all of us in our spiritual inventories, that there is always something for us to fix?"

Anticipating the question that was to follow, the Baal Shem Tov continued, "And on occasion Hashem sends us messages through non-Jews as well."

The Toldos, with undisguised frustration, answered, "Absolutely not! I can't accept such a concept."

"Of course you can," responded the Baal Shem Tov. "You just don't want to."

The Toldos left in an agitated state of mind, his thoughts churning over what had just transpired. He was jolted out of his thinking by a gentile wagon driver, standing by his overturned wagon, who called out to him, "*Yid*, come over here and help me get these bales of hay back on the wagon."

Reflexively, the Toldos replied, "I'm sorry, I can't."

The wagon driver sneered, "Of course you can; you just don't want to."

Hearing the Baal Shem Tov's words echoed back to him so immediately was just too much to be chalked up to coincidence, and the rest is history...

Examples of Heavenly communications abound on a daily basis in all of our lives.

Consider the following:

A distant cousin, Perry, the daughter of a distinguished rabbinic family, had recently suffered the loss of her father, a wise and loving man. As she was processing her grief, she entered the always stressful chapter of *shidduchim* with one of her daughters. Try as she might, she could not make up her mind about a certain match that was suggested for her daughter. The young man in question had many positive qualities, but being that her daughter was so super-special, Perry wasn't sure that this *bochur* could do her justice. Should she be satisfied with "well enough," she questioned, or should she hold out for someone more extraordinary?

Previously, with her older children, Perry had been able to consult with her father, who was a very decisive individual. Now, in his absence, she was at a total loss, suspended in a state of doubt. Perry related that, in desperation, she went into the family room, closed the lights, and sat down on her recliner to try to sort out her feelings.

From the next room, she overheard her children discussing their friends. Eli described his friend (this particular "*bochur*") as extraordinary, while Moshe insisted that though he did not think him to be "extra" ordinary in the same way Eli did, he was, nonetheless, special in that he was a truly caring person, a lot of fun, and wonderful to be with.

Perry was blown away. Hashem, through His messengers in the universe, had sent her the answer. What made the "message" even more providential was that it contained elements that were unmistakably Heaven-sent. Perry confided that during her earlier issues with *shidduchim*, she would call her father and say, "Tatty, they are suggesting this extraordinary *shidduch* for me."

Invariably her father's response would be "*Tochter* (my dear daughter), don't look for extraordinary. Extraordinary usually comes with extraordinary problems. Instead, try to find someone wonderful, with good character and *middos tovos*, but ordinary."

No longer in doubt, Perry understood her marching orders and proceeded to embrace the wonderful, "ordinary" young man with a full heart.

And how about this? My friend, Devorah, struggled with sleep problems for many years. Primarily, she was afflicted with something called "restless leg syndrome," a not-uncommon condition that compromises people's ability to get a good night's rest.

On one occasion, one of Devorah's associates insisted that Devorah accompany her while she went to have her nails done. Despite her busy schedule and not particularly enamored with nail salons, Devorah charitably conceded. While waiting for her friend, Devorah overheard a conversation from the cubicle next to her. (Beauty parlors and *sheitel machers* are typically places where people share, and perhaps over-share, personal information about their lives.)

The woman adjacent to her was complaining about her insomnia, identifying the cause of her sleeplessness as restless leg syndrome.

"Wow, what a coincidence," the beautician replied. "I've suffered from that ever since I was a teenager. My doctor prescribed this fabulous medication, and I haven't been bothered by it since."

Needless to say, Devorah followed up, and the medicine helped her immensely. A nail salon and an overheard conversation?

"Hashem truly does love me," concluded Devorah.

Coincidences, cynics may claim, but for all of us who know better, messages orchestrated from above abound, and hopefully we will keep listening.

Yankele, our three-year-old great-grandson, is a particularly gifted child. As described earlier, this young philosopher once pointed out to his mother, "Isn't it true, Mommy, that we can see Hashem much better in the dark than in the light?"

Yankele has a point on many levels. The one relevant to our discussion is that during our daily routine there are so many distractions, so much vying for our attention, that we become oblivious to Hashem's communications. We are hurried and hassled. It is not until night casts its blanket over our busy-ness that we can contemplate the day's events and what they are telling us. Unfortunately, by then we have passed up many messages, forgotten the events that transmitted them, and are usually too tired to think straight. Slowing down to listen and pick up on Hashem's messages as they become manifest, moment to moment during the day, is a formidable challenge.

A writer of note expressed it very aptly when she said, "Days pass and years vanish and we walk sightless among miracles." Our entreaty to Hashem should be, "*Ribbono Shel Olam,* fill our eyes with seeing and our minds with knowing. Let there be moments when Your Presence, like lightning, illuminates the darkness in which we walk. Help us to see wherever we gaze that the bush burns unconsumed and that we, clay touched by Your Will, reach out for holiness and exclaim in wonder, 'How filled with awe is this place and we did not know it.'"

Conclusion

My dear readers, in the life of the Jew there are no endings; indeed when one door closes, another opens. This concept is captured by the practice we observe on Simchas Torah, wherein as soon as we complete the reading of the last *parshah* of the Torah, *V'zos Haberachah*, we take out another Torah scroll and begin from the first *parshah*, the *"sedra"* Bereishis. We begin anew; the cycle of life continues. Indeed, regardless how extensive our accomplishments, as bearers of a Divine *neshamah* we all have "miles to go before we sleep." My blessing and wish to all of you is that Hashem may bless *Klal Yisrael* in general, and each one of us individually, with continued success on our joint journey toward excellence and redemption.

About the Author

Rebbetzin Feige Twerski is the mother of eleven children and many grandchildren whose number she refuses to divulge. Alongside her husband, Rabbi Michel Twerski, *shlita*, she serves as Rebbetzin to her community in Milwaukee and counsels people all over the globe. The Rebbetzin is a popular lecturer, speaking on a wide variety of topics to audiences in America and overseas. She is the author of *Ask Rebbetzin Feige* and *Rebbetzin Feige Responds* (both published by Artscroll).

About Mosaica Press

Mosaica Press is an independent publisher of Jewish books. Our authors include some of the most profound, interesting, and entertaining thinkers and writers in the Jewish community today. There is a great demand for high-quality Jewish works dealing with issues of the day — and Mosaica Press is helping fill that need. Our books are available around the world. Please visit us at **www.mosaicapress.com** or contact us at **info@mosaicapress.com**. We will be glad to hear from you.

MOSAICA PRESS